THE DISCIPLINES OF A DISCIPLE

The Disciplines of a Disciple

John Bertolucci
with
Fred Lilly

SERVANT BOOKS
Ann Arbor, Michigan

Available from Servant Publications, Box 8617,
   Ann Arbor, Michigan 48107

ISBN 0-89283-240-1
Printed in the United States of America

85 86 87 88 89   10 9 8 7 6 5 4 3 2 1

CONTENTS

ONE

"Follow Me"

T HE NIGHT AIR was hot and steamy. Smells of fish and mildew hung low over the beaches along the lake of Gennesaret. Flies swarmed near the shoreline, and small animals crept towards the lake for their evening watering.

The fishermen from Bethsaida began assembling at their boats. They were hearty men, accustomed to working at night, because fish were easier to catch in the dark than during the light of day. The word was out that this would be a hard night. Not only was it hot and still, but early fishing parties reported that the fishing was not going to be good.

Simon and Andrew, two brothers, prepared their nets, their boats, and the other equipment they needed to go after the night's catch. They worked slowly, carefully. They gradually became aware that something was different about this night. Perhaps God would speak to them. They were spiritual men after all. They were faithful Israelites. They honored the sabbath and tried to live according to the spiritual laws which had been handed down to them.

As they expected, the fishing wasn't good. Simon and Andrew stayed out for hours, dragging their nets through the places in the lake where they usually found large schools of fish. Their partners, James and John, had been out in their own boat with their father, Zebedee. They hadn't had much luck either.

Shortly after dawn the fishermen rowed back to shore. They were dejectedly cleaning their nets on the beach when they noticed a crowd gathered around a young stranger. The man was speaking to the crowd. The fishermen couldn't hear what he was saying and, though they were curious, the nets had to be cleaned, so they continued to work.

Simon was about finished with his work when he heard the man's voice. He was very close now. He seemed to be talking about God. "A rabbi's son," he thought, "trying to impress everyone with his learning."

But as he listened Simon became intrigued.

"He doesn't sound like any rabbi's son I've ever heard. He's not showing off at all. He really seems to know a lot about God. I've never heard a rabbi talk like that. I wonder who this man is?"

Suddenly the man turned, stepped into the boat and addressed Simon and Andrew.

"Row out from shore," he said.

Simon and Andrew were startled by the command.

But they picked up the oars, got into the boat, and began rowing. The stranger continued talking to the crowd about what he called "the reign of God." He talked about God as if the Most High really cared what happened to people. He said that God had sent him to preach some "good news" to the people of Israel.

"I could use some good news right now," Simon thought. "I wonder if he knows where the fish are."

After a few moments the young man finished preaching and dismissed the crowd. Then he turned to Simon and Andrew.

"Put out into deep water and lower your nets for a catch," he said.

Simon detected authority in the voice. "Strange," he thought. "I wonder how he knew my thoughts."

"Master," Simon said, "we have been hard at it all night long and have caught nothing; but if you say so, I will lower the nets."

So the brothers rowed out into the deep water and lowered their nets. Immediately, the nets were filled with fish, so many fish that the nets were ready to burst. Simon and Andrew were unable to haul them back into the boat.

"Come help us," they shouted to James and John who were watching from their boat which was anchored near the beach.

The stranger watched with an amused smile on his face while the four fishermen hauled in the heavy nets. There were so many fish that both boats looked as if they were going to sink. The fishermen were so tired when they finished that they barely had the strength to row back to shore.

After catching his breath and evaluating the great catch of fish, Simon realized that the stranger in his boat was indeed no ordinary man. He crawled through the piles of fish and fell to his knees at the feet of Jesus.

Overcome with astonishment and fear, Simon said, "Leave me, Lord. I am a sinful man."

Andrew rubbed his aching arms and watched his brother half kneeling and half laying in the pile of slimy fish.

"Sometimes I want to hide when Simon begins to make a fool of himself," he thought. "But my brother is not so foolish right now. If I had his courage I'd be lying in the fish, too. This man claims to speak for God, and everything I've seen makes me believe he's telling the truth. I can't wait to hear him speak again."

James and John sat in the next boat amazed by the unfolding drama. They watched their friend Simon, always the one to act without thinking things through, address the stranger in words that were reserved for the holiest priests in Jerusalem.

"Simon often makes a fool of himself," John thought as the boat carrying he and his brother began to drift towards dry land. "But this time I think he's right. That's no ordinary man, and this is no ordinary catch of fish. I've heard of the Lord's power at work through our fathers, but I've never seen it happen. Now I'm certain that the Holy One is working wonders through him."

"Who do you think he is?" James asked in a hushed voice.

"He's one of God's holy prophets," John replied. "No ordinary man can say the things he says and do the works he does without God's favor. I've been hearing about him for many days. His name is Jesus. John the baptizer told us to listen carefully to all he has to say. I hear that he has been going around the district preaching and healing diseases. He's even driven out demons. His powers seem to be unlimited."

"I don't know if he's a prophet or not," James answered. "But he certainly has powers. And when he talks about the Most High my heart is filled with joy. I've never felt this way before. He makes me want to dance and sing and pray all at the same time. Let's follow him today and see what he does."

"I've been thinking the same thing," John said. "The hired men will help our father clean these fish. I know that I have to follow this man. He is God's chosen one and I have no choice but to hear all that he has to say."

In the other boat Simon continued to lie in the fish. He was frightened and confused, but he had never felt so right about anything in his life. He knew that he had to humble himself before one who demonstrated a power that can only come from the Most High God.

After several minutes of quiet, Jesus put his hand on Simon's head and said, "Do not be afraid. From now on you will be catching men just as you caught these fish." Then he instructed them to row back to shore.

The fishermen returned to shore and dragged their

heavy boats out of the water. As they did so, Jesus got out of Simon's boat and began to walk away. The two pairs of brothers looked at each other and individually made the silent decision to follow him. James hesitated a moment, looking at Zebedee sitting a few yards away on the beach. Then he looked at John and Simon and Andrew who were walking after Jesus.

"I've got to go, too," he thought. With that he turned from his father and began running towards his brother and the one who had set his heart on fire.

Jesus spent the next few days leading his new disciples through town after town in the region of Galilee. When they were alone he explained his mission to them, quoting from the prophets, especially from the great prophet Isaiah. But quiet moments were few during those days, for Jesus was pursued by great crowds bringing the sick for him to heal.

The disciples watched as many of those who were sick were healed indeed. But the most amazing things that happened during those days were occurring in their hearts. The more Jesus explained the writings of the prophets, the more the disciples became convinced that he did really come from God. Their hearts burned within them as he spoke. The more they were with him, the more they loved him. They no longer desired to return to their village and their fishing boats.

One evening the sons of Zebedee took leave of the group of disciples and talked about their future.

"If we continue to follow Jesus, does that mean that

we have abandoned our father?" James asked. "We cannot abandon him. That would not be right. Our law tells us to honor our father."

"I know it sounds like a terrible thing," John replied. "God's law tells us to obey our father and honor him. I don't want to abandon him. But I know that I have to follow Jesus and learn more about this good news he says the Holy One sent him to proclaim. I hope you stay with me, James. We can return home from time to time and help our father.

"I have an idea. Let's go to our father's house tomorrow and talk this over with him."

The next morning the brothers set out for Zebedee's house. But James, who had talked with Jesus during the night, no longer felt guilty about leaving Zebedee.

"The Most High wants us to follow his servant Jesus," the brothers told their father and mother, and they went on to tell their parents about everything that had happened.

Zebedee didn't know what to make of his sons' story. He was angry about being left to support the family and supervise the hired men by himself. But his sons were going; he knew there was no point in arguing. So he blessed them and wished them well.

A few days later the brothers were following Jesus through a town when he suddenly stopped and called to a man sitting nearby. The man's name was Levi. The people of the town hated him because he collected taxes for the Romans. Peter became tense as Jesus approached Levi. A crowd gathered as they talked.

"Who are you and what do you want with me?" Levi asked.

Jesus held him with his gaze for several minutes. Then he said, "Follow me."

Peter watched in amazement as Levi turned his back on his office and the stack of money sitting there in plain view and followed Jesus who was walking away. Jesus motioned to the disciples to move away so that he could speak with Levi. After a while Levi left, and Jesus returned to the place where his disciples were sitting in the shade of a tree.

"We will stay at Levi's house tonight," he said.

Levi, meanwhile, was going around the town inviting everyone he met to come to his house that night to hear Jesus. "He's changed my life," Levi said. "Come listen to him and he'll change yours too! He speaks with the authority of a prophet of the Most High."

Because Levi worked in league with the hated Romans and was known to cheat people as well, he didn't get many positive responses to his dinner invitations. But the poor of the town, knowing that Levi could put a good meal on the table, came to the banquet.

That night the fishermen, accustomed to having Jesus to themselves much of the time, found that they were being ignored as the tax collectors and the poor of the town pushed close to their Master. Simon looked on resentfully as Levi sat smiling next to Jesus and listened to him speak.

Some Pharisees were also present, looking very skeptical and ill at ease, but still managing to eat a good bit of food. Finally one of them stood and challenged Jesus. "Why, if you claim to be a servant of the Holy One," he asked, "are you dining with these sinners and outcasts? If you really were the servant of the Holy One, you would be in Jerusalem feasting with the chief priests."

Jesus looked at the man and those with him. Firmly but gently he replied, "The healthy do not need a doctor; sick people do. I have not come to invite the self-righteous to a change of heart, but sinners."

The Pharisee looked as if he wanted to argue, but Jesus' gaze had reduced him to silence. Blushing, he quickly sat town.

When the meal was finished and the guests began to leave, Jesus came over to Simon and corrected him for his rash judgment concerning Levi.

"Forgive me, Master," Simon pleaded. "I have walked with you these many days, I have heard your teaching and seen the power of God come forth from your hands. I have been changed in so many ways. But the old Simon keeps cropping up.

"I shall go at once to Levi and repent for my judgment. I gladly welcome him to our band if you have chosen him to walk with us."

And so Peter spent much of the nighttime hours listening to Levi tell his story.

"It is not easy being a tax collector," Levi said. "When I walk down the street people ignore me or they say hateful things to me. Sometimes they even throw things at me. I cannot even go to the synagogue. The moment I walk in a disruption begins.

"I got into this business because of the money I knew I could make. But after losing all my friends I realized the money was not worth the pain. How many times I have wanted to leave it all behind, to become an ordinary merchant or to work with my hands. But I found out that I was trapped. Everyone hates me now. They'd never patronize Levi the merchant or Levi the tradesman.

"But when your Master walked by the customs house this morning and called to me, all my old fears disappeared. He has such a way about him. I don't know how to explain what happened. I just knew that if I followed him today, I could have a new chance in life. He offered me a new life, and I would have been a fool to refuse it."

Peter, James, John, Andrew, and Levi. Five men called by Jesus Christ to be his first disciples. Later they would be joined by other men and women, all of whom selflessly dedicated themselves to the man who did such extraordinary things in the name of God.

Jesus calls men and women today, too. Sometimes the call is as dramatic as Simon Peter in his boat or Levi in his customs house. Sometimes the call is much quieter. But it is the same Lord who calls and for the same reason—to make us disciples capable of being skilled "fishers of men."

TWO

"The Kingdom of God"

E VERY TIME I READ IT I am amazed anew by St. Luke's account of the call of the first disciples. Jesus took these simple fishermen, the hated tax collector, and a few others, taught them about the "kingdom of God," and sent them out into the world to turn it upside down. They played a vitally important role in God's plan for the human race.

These men, and the dozens of men and women who were to join the ranks of Jesus' disciples during his public ministry, had a great privilege. They were discipled by the living Word of God. Day after day they walked with him and ate with him and laughed and cried with him. And all the while he was teaching them, drawing them on to spiritual maturity so that they could haul "great catches" of men and women into God's kingdom.

We do not have the same privilege of experiencing the Word of God alive in the flesh. We do, however, have the opportunity to be discipled by that same Word of God—Jesus Christ our Lord. He has filled Christians with his Holy Spirit so that we can be his disciples. As we surrender our lives to him, turn to him in prayer, read his word in the scriptures, and experience the power of his Holy Spirit in the church, we become his disciples just like the men who left their fishing boats to follow the Christ.

The teachings of the scriptures and the church teach us a great deal about being disciples of Jesus Christ. Through them the Holy Spirit speaks to us about following Jesus in a very personal way. By reading, studying, and reflecting on God's word, we can have the privilege of being taught and led on to Christian maturity by the same Jesus who taught the disciples of old.

Who can be a disciple? Jesus did not at first seek out the well-educated and highly-gifted of his day. He sought out ordinary people to be his first disciples. Of course he wanted the gifted ones to believe the good news and experience new life in him, but the vast majority of his disciples were ordinary people.

Jesus continues to work in a similar way in our day. He seeks out all, especially ordinary people—the housewife, the student, the factory worker, the insurance salesman. He seeks out the educated and the gifted too, but he wants all of us to be disciples. He issues his call to all of us just where we are, just as he did to Simon, Andrew, James, John, and Levi.

All over the world we are seeing a growing trend: the

Lord Jesus Christ is calling men and women to become his disciples in a very personal way. Men and women are responding by the tens of thousands, especially in the poor countries of the Third World, but also in the nations of the West. It is a very exciting time in the history of God's people.

What kind of men and women are responding to God's call? Some are very familiar, like the Christian athletes and television personalities who are famous for their commitment to Christ. But equally impressive are the stories of college students, married couples, retired people, and others who have experienced the love of Jesus in their lives and have responded enthusiastically to his call to become disciples.

The first step in growing as a disciple of the Lord is to understand what discipleship means.

The word "disciple" comes from the same root word as "discipline." "Discipline" means much more than punishment. It means instruction or training in a particular field of study. Discipline usually does involve correction and sometimes involves punishment. But these are only done to contribute to the effort of training the person being corrected.

A disciple, then, is a person disciplined—trained—by Jesus Christ to be a servant of God. Disciples join in God's great plan of salvation of the human race by serving as evangelists, teachers, pastors, prophets, intercessors, missionaries, administrators, church janitors, and in many other roles.

When we understand what a disciple is, we can then

understand how the process of discipleship begins. Jesus calls his disciples personally. He calls us by name, not just as members of a Christian body. He calls us individually and with a deep respect for our individual personalities. God tells us, "I have called you by name and you are mine" (Is 43:1).

Just as God calls each of his disciples personally, he knows them intimately. In fact, he knows us better than we know ourselves. He knows everything about our background, the culture we were raised in, our ancestry, our families. And most important, he knows and cares about everything that has happened to us since the moment we were conceived in our mothers' wombs. Scripture says:

The Lord called me from birth, from my mother's womb he gave me my name.... Can a mother forget her infant, be without tenderness for the child of her womb? Even should she forget, I will never forget you. See, upon the palms of my hands I have written your name. (Is 49:1, 15-16)

God loves each of us intimately and cares for us completely. Therefore, when we experience his call to be disciples, there is no reason to fear unworthiness. God knows all about us. He knows what he needs to do to change us. All we have to do is accept his call, and he will give us everything we need to accomplish his purposes for our lives.

How do you know when God is calling you to

discipleship? It's not as difficult to know as it may sound. God's call is no mystical thing. He usually makes his will known quite plainly. For many people the call to discipleship is a gradual realization that God has a particular area of service in mind for them. For others the call is a sudden, clear revelation often experienced during prayer.

Take my friend Margaret, for example. She experienced a gradual shift in priorities and outlook until she had dedicated her life to the service of the Lord. Many people are like her.

Margaret grew up in a Catholic home and attended Catholic schools. She was not exactly a model child, but she was fortunate enough not to be interested in the rebellion that swept up many young people growing up in the 1960s and early 70s. Margaret had no interest in drugs or "free love." She and her friends enjoyed studying together. They spent their leisure time camping and working on arts and crafts.

During her high school and early college years Margaret spent most of her Sunday afternoons and Tuesday evenings preparing children in her parish to receive the sacraments. In fact, she was as involved as many adults in the religious education program in her parish.

With adulthood, however, Margaret sensed that God expected more from her. He had given her talents and abilities, and she knew that he expected a greater share of her time and energy to be devoted to his work. So she began attending Mass more often than just on

Sunday. She dedicated some quiet time each evening to prayer for God's direction in her life. Gradually, God's will began to unfold for Margaret. He showed her that his plan for her life was marriage and motherhood. He showed her that he had given her a special gift to love and teach children and mothers of young children.

Margaret responded to God's gradual and gentle call. She married and gave birth to several children. Even though she was busy caring for her own husband and children, and even though she had to work part-time to bring home much needed extra income, she still made the time to be faithful to the call God had placed on her life.

When a woman needed a listening ear, a helping hand, or some practical advice, Margaret was always available. She was often the first person a fellow parishioner in need called because they knew they would get not only sympathy and prayer, but some practical advice as well.

Margaret's story is a common one. There are many such Christian women. The vocation of wife and mother and sister to Christians in need is a vital one in God's church. There are many other Christian women who take more noticeable roles in the leadership of God's people. Both are valuable. Both are necessary. Both are real discipleship roles.

Have you been called to be a disciple of the Lord? If you are a committed, practicing Christian then the answer is yes! I believe that God calls all Christian people who have committed their lives to Christ to be his disciples. Remember Jesus' parable of the talents? God has given each person gifts and talents, and he expects them to be used wisely and carefully for the building up of the body of Christ.

The process of discipleship starts with a decision. And right now I ask you to consider this basic call of following the Lord. Have you made that all-important decision? Do you hear him calling you personally and by name? Have you come to grips with what is to be your most basic identity—that you belong to Jesus Christ? That he is the very center of your life?

Right now God is calling each of you who have not accepted his call, who have not said that "yes" to the Lord, to consider doing so. If you are such a person and you wish to surrender your life to Jesus and become his disciple, enter now into a spirit of prayer, and say this simple, humble prayer:

"O Lord my God, I know that you love me with an everlasting love. I know that you have created me as a unique human being. There is no other like me in all your creation. I also know that I am a sinner, that I have fallen short of fulfilling the purposes you have created me for. But I want to be a follower of Jesus Christ, your only Son and my Lord. I want to be his disciple. I say yes right now to your call to discipleship. Send your Holy Spirit upon me that I may begin to learn all that Jesus has for me as his disciple. Thank you, Father. Praise you, Jesus. Come, Holy Spirit. Amen."

I know some people who prayed that kind of prayer and made that kind of commitment years ago. Yet, they are frustrated today by what they see as a lack of fruitfulness in their spiritual lives and ministry. Let's take a look at what happened to them and some of the remedies they need to apply. This will help the new disciple avoid some pitfalls in his walk with the Lord. For many Christians who are stuck in a rut, it will point the way out.

THREE

Stuck in a Rut

JOHN AND YVONNE EXPERIENCED spiritual renewal in their lives twelve years ago. At that time they had been married for five years and the concerns of earning a living and raising a family had just about eclipsed everything else in their lives. They went to church on Sundays, but aside from that one hour a week, neither had an active spiritual life.

Then one day a couple who lived down the street told John and Yvonne that they had received the "baptism in the Holy Spirit." They had been on the verge of divorce, and the minister who was counseling them told them about the charismatic renewal and prayed for them. Their marriage had been saved, their lives redirected, and now they were telling all their friends about Jesus Christ and this gift of the Holy Spirit.

John and Yvonne were interested. They began

attending prayer meetings at the couple's house. After a few meetings they too received the gift of the Holy Spirit. Immediately their lives began to change. Until then their jobs and their nice home had been the first priority in their lives. Now learning more about Christ came first. Instead of sitting in front of the TV at night, they read the Bible. Instead of going to parties or working late, they went to prayer meetings, Christian banquets, church services and conferences.

After about a year John and Yvonne decided to start a prayer group in their Catholic parish. The pastor gave them his permission and even allowed them to use a room in the parish social center for prayer meetings. The prayer group grew steadily for four years. It had started with only two couples and two nuns who taught at the parish school. Within six months, twenty-five people were atttending the prayer meetings each week. A year later they grew even larger when they merged with a group that had been meeting in private homes.

As the numbers grew, so did the spiritual activities. Teenagers started attending the meetings, and so a Bible study for young people was started. Women began meeting together in small groups during the day, and men began having breakfast or lunch with one another. Families in the prayer group wanted to be with other families, so several kinds of social activities were scheduled.

In a few years the group had grown from six people to more than a hundred. It had an excellent music group, a teaching ministry, a core of dedicated leaders, and pastoral guidance from two priests and a Pentecostal minister.

Yet all was not well. The enthusiasm of members slowly began to wane. The numbers of visitors began to drop off. First one priest dropped out and then the other. Disagreements about leadership developed. Some people left the Catholic church to join a local independent charismatic congregation. After only four years, things were falling apart.

The group still meets, but on a good day only twenty people come to the weekly prayer meeting. Many of the most dedicated members were burned out by activities in the parish and rarely attend today. John and Yvonne are perplexed. They don't understand why the group fizzled.

But they haven't given up. They know what God did in their own lives, and they believe that he intends to use the prayer group to reach others. They are patiently persevering, even though it is painful to do so. It would have been so much easier to quit. But the perseverance has come at great cost. Their own spiritual lives seem to suffer. Their bewilderment over what happened grows instead of lessens. They need help and have no idea where to find it.

Marsha's story is different but her need is the same. She is a single woman in her late thirties. She has always wanted to marry, but the right man has never come along. All her friends married and she has slowly drifted away from all but one of them, a woman named

Jenny who is married to a successful businessman. Jenny began attending prayer luncheons sponsored by an interdenominational women's group, and she invited Marsha to join her. Marsha did, but was turned off by some of the things she experienced there. She stopped attending, but she feels a spiritual hunger and she has no idea what to do about it.

Marsha's church is typical of many. They have nice Sunday services, a Bible study on Wednesday night, courses in Christian doctrine for adults, and programs for every need from alcoholics anonymous to social service for the needy. Marsha is involved in some of these things, but they do not meet her spiritual needs. She wants to grow closer to Christ, but no one can tell her how to do it.

Robert has still a different kind of need. He grew up in a lively Christian home. His parents were active in their church, and Robert decided to follow Christ at an early age. After a short period of rebellion against the faith of his childhood, he experienced a fresh conversion while in college.

Today Robert is a successful Christian man. He built a small but profitable business and trained capable people to run it for him. He has lots of free time, which he uses for Christian work. Robert is a charming man and a good speaker. He spends many an evening giving talks before church groups throughout the state. He developed an evangelism program that is so successful that he has appeared on Christian television programs to share it with others. His story has been told in a book. The book was not a best seller, but a few thousand people have been inspired by it.

As successful as he is, however, Robert has a great spiritual need. He has yet to sink deep Christian roots. He has belonged to three different churches, even though he has lived in the same house for twenty years. His prayer life is undisciplined. His wife and children resent the fact that he rarely spends time with them.

What do John and Yvonne, Marsha and Robert have in common? They have all experienced Christ in their lives. They became aware of the great revival that is occurring today and have tried to become part of it. But each of these people is stuck in a rut. For John and Yvonne the rut is being part of a spiritual renewal movement which peaked very quickly and seems to be going nowhere. They have yet to discover what the next step is.

Marsha is isolated in a church that is perhaps holding its own, but apparently not moving forward. Like her church, Marsha is in danger of falling into a pattern of slow spiritual death.

Robert is a victim of individualism. He has failed to establish some basic building blocks of Christian living and has yet to discover his mistake.

Each of these people, and every other Christian in a similar rut, needs to learn or to relearn how to be a true disciple of Jesus Christ. They need to come under the direction of the one Lord as did the disciples in New

Testament times. For many such people the remedy is to return to their spiritual roots. They need to recall again what Jesus Christ did in their lives when their faith first came alive. They need to return again to their "first love" (Rv 2:4-5).

The place to start is in the house of a Pharisee named Simon.

FOUR

A New Way of Life

O NE EVENING A PROSTITUTE named Mary was walking along a muddy street, hoping that the rain
would let up so that she could find a man to purchase
her services for the evening. The rain didn't stop,
however, so she decided to go inside where it was dry
and wait for the weather to clear.

With that, she headed home. Turning a corner she
noticed a large crowd of people in front of the house of
a wealthy merchant, a man who also belonged to the
religious party of the Pharisees.

"What's going on here?" Mary demanded. A few
people in the back of the crowd turned towards her,
but turned quickly away in disgust when they saw who
had spoken.

"I asked what's going on here," Mary shouted.

"It's the man Jesus," someone answered without
looking at her. "He's dining here in Simon's house."

"Jesus," Mary exclaimed. "I've heard about him.

They say he has been healing people of diseases and casting out demons. I want to hear him."

Mary shoved her way through the crowd, but could not reach the door. She did, however, hear others talking about Jesus.

"He healed my crippled nephew," one woman said.

"Oh, sure," scoffed another. "You're just saying that to make us all think you're something special."

"All I know," the first woman said, "is that my dear sister brought her son to where Jesus was preaching and he healed the boy. He's been unable to walk these ten years of his life. And now he can run and jump and play with the other children. He's even begun to learn his father's trade so he won't have to be a beggar."

"My husband and I were unable to get along with each other for years," another woman said. "We argued and he beat me. I saw Jesus preaching one day and I stopped to listen. He told me my sins were forgiven. When he did, I felt all the hatred leave me. I've hated my husband and myself for so many years, I forgot what it was like to be happy. With those few words Jesus set me free of all that. Even my husband has forgiven me and has stopped beating me. Jesus is wonderful, a real prophet of God."

Mary turned and pushed her way back through the crowd and fell to her knees out in the street. "I have heard many stories about this Jesus," she thought. "When that woman spoke about her sins being forgiven, well . . . I hate myself too. I wonder, Jesus, will you forgive me? Will God rescue me from this mess my life is in if I hear those words from your lips?"

Suddenly, Mary was overcome by a strange, but peaceful presence. It was as if God was indeed speaking to her, telling her to go to Jesus.

"I will, I will," Mary mumbled. She got to her feet and began running to her home. She flung open the door and ran to a cabinet where she stored her perfumed oil. "I've paid good money for this," she thought. "I'll give it to Jesus. I hope it is a fitting gift for him. If I show him I am sorry for my sins, I am sure he will forgive me and I can experience peace. I wonder what it will be like? I haven't known peace since I was a child. I'm not so sure I even knew it then."

Mary rushed back out into the street and headed to Simon's house once again. Arriving there she shoved her way through the crowd, which had grown even larger. She used the jar of perfume to push people out of the way and was not at all deterred by the insults and the blows she received in return. She pushed past the servant at the door and rushed into the room where Jesus was dining. She fell to her knees at his feet. Weeping with joy at seeing Jesus, Mary let her tears fall upon his feet. Then she wiped them with her long hair, kissed them, and poured the perfumed oil on them. Jesus placed his hand on Mary's head, but said nothing.

Simon the Pharisee, and the other guests at the table, looked on in horror. "If this man were indeed a prophet," Simon thought, "he would know who and what sort of woman this is that touches him—that she is a sinner."

Jesus knew what Simon was thinking. He told the Pharisee a story. Two men owed a certain moneylender different amounts of money. One owed the lender a great deal, and one only a small amount. Neither man was able to repay the loan; each asked the lender to forgive the debt. He forgave both.

"Which of them was more grateful to the moneylender?" Jesus asked.

"He, I presume, to whom he remitted the larger sum," Simon answered.

"You are right," Jesus said.

Then he motioned towards Mary. "You see this woman? I came to your home and you provided me with no water for my feet. She has washed my feet with her tears and wiped them with her hair. You gave me no kiss, but she has not ceased kissing my feet since I entered. You did not anoint my head with oil, but she has anointed my feet with perfume. I tell you, that is why her many sins are forgiven—because of her great love. Little is forgiven the one whose love is small."

Then Jesus looked into Mary's eyes and said, "Your sins are forgiven."

With those words, Mary's heart overflowed with joy, and the tears began to flow freely from her eyes once again.

"Thank you, thank you, Jesus," she stuttered through her tears.

Simon and his guests, however, were aghast. "Who is this that even forgives sins?" they asked one another.

Jesus ignored them and continued speaking to Mary. "Your faith has been your salvation," he said. "Now go in peace."

Mary stumbled out of the house and through the crowd, crying and shouting, "I'm free; I'm free."

From that night on she vowed that she would never again sin as she had in her past. Instead, she began to follow Jesus and the disciples and serve them in any way she could.

Mary became a great heroine of the Christian faith. She joined a small group of other women who donated money to the apostles, fed them, and encouraged others to hear Jesus' preaching. These first women disciples came to the Lord in a similar way. They heard him preach, they experienced a conversion in their hearts because of his words, and they began living a new way of life based on their faith in him and their adherence to his teaching.

Mary and the other women did not live with Jesus as the twelve apostles did, but they came to listen to Jesus and to serve him whenever they could. They knew that they needed to return to Jesus again and again to partake ever more deeply of the new life he had to offer.

We modern disciples need to learn that lesson also. The life which the Lord has for us is so vast and so deep that we can never partake of it fully—there is always more of it to receive. It is, in fact, eternal life. Life that never ends. It only gets fuller and deeper as each year passes, and it spills over into eternal life after we leave these mortal bodies.

Some wise Christian teachers have said that the life a disciple lives is like really beginning heaven on earth. The life of prayer, of listening to the Lord, of worshiping him and finding deep joy in his presence is what heaven is all about.

An awareness of the presence, the power, and the glory of the Lord is intended by God to be a normal part of every Christian's faith experience. Millions of people the world over have experienced the power of the Holy Spirit in their lives in a dramatic new way since this spiritual movement began sometime during the middle of our century.

To some, the experience is one of entering a new and dynamic personal relationship with Jesus Christ. Those Christians in what are called Evangelical churches usually call this experience being "born again."

To others, the experience is one not only of a profound relationship with Jesus, but includes the added dimension of spiritual power. These people have witnessed miracles, healings, prophecy, and speaking in tongues. They are part of what is called Pentecostalism or charismatic renewal; they say they have received the "baptism in the Holy Spirit."

What do I mean by baptism in the Holy Spirit? Simply speaking, it is to be immersed in the Spirit of Jesus Christ in such a way that our whole life is changed. Theologically speaking, it is allowing the graces of baptism and confirmation to be stirred up in our lives.

Some people say that baptism in the Holy Spirit and charismatic renewal are just for some Christians. I do not agree. I believe that everyone in the church—every man, woman, and child—is called to experience a full life in the Holy Spirit. This is what we call the baptism in the Holy Spirit.

There are different ways of experiencing this phenomenon; there are different ways of describing it, different terms for it, and different ways of living out the implications of this experience. But Jesus Christ made it clear when he spoke to his disciples after his resurrection that they were to receive the full promise of the Father—the full power of the Holy Spirit. This applies to us every bit as much as it did to the apostles.

I believe that the Holy Spirit will come upon us in the twentieth century just as he came on the men and women of the first century. He can come upon us in a very deep and powerful way. We pray for this in the liturgy. Every time we come together to celebrate the Eucharist, we pray that everyone who partakes of the Body and Blood of the Lord is filled with the Holy Spirit.

There is a traditional prayer based on Psalm 104:30 that Catholics have been praying for centuries: "Come Holy Spirit, fill the hearts of your faithful and enkindle in us the fire of divine love. Send forth your Spirit and we shall be recreated." When Catholics pray that prayer, we are asking for Jesus to give us the baptism of the Holy Spirit.

However you approach this spiritual reality of the infilling of the Holy Spirit, whatever you call it, you should want to experience a new Pentecost in your life. You should want to be filled with the Spirit as the apostles were on the first Pentecost, and as so many in the church have been in our own time.

This reality of receiving the Holy Spirit, of yielding to the Holy Spirit, of being baptized by the Holy Spirit, is the way the Lord Jesus Christ continues to disciple us. He said to us, before he left us to ascend to the Father: "Behold, I am with you always, until the end of the world" (Mt 28:20). How is he with us? Through the power, the presence, the action of the Holy Spirit in our lives.

He continues to disciple us through the Holy Spirit just as he sat down and formed the disciples he chose while on earth. He taught them; he corrected them; he molded them into the men and women who would lead his church in its earliest days. After his ascension, he began to teach, correct, and mold men and women— through the infilling of the Holy Spirit. He has continued to do this down through the ages, especially in our day in the worldwide outpouring of the Holy Spirit we are seeing in every land on earth.

Even Christians who find it hard to identify with the "born again" Evangelicals and the "Spirit baptized" Pentecostals, are still experiencing a renewal of spiritual vitality. In most Christian churches great developments in Christian service, theology, and ecumenical activity are taking place. Many Christians have decided that caring for the poor, or working for reforms in government, or defending the right to life of unborn babies is a necessary part of living the message of the gospel. Other kinds of service ministries are flourishing as men and women turn their hearts over to God.

Each of these is an example of the new way of living Jesus has for his disciples. When Jesus comes into our lives, we experience not only love and grace but a desire to serve. This is because the new way of living calls for a radical response from us. Mary Magdalene was a changed woman after her encounter with Jesus Christ. We should be changed people too every time we encounter him, especially the time we turn our lives over to him and receive his new life.

Jesus desires to teach his disciples a way of life that is radically different from the life we live in the world. In fact, the way of life of a disciple of Christ is in *opposition* to the way most people live today. The call to discipleship is a radical call to a life of sacrifice, hard work, and also joys beyond imagining.

St. Paul says it this way in a passage from his Epistle to the Ephesians:

I declare and solemnly attest in the Lord that you must no longer live as the pagans do—their minds empty, their understanding darkened. They are estranged from a life in God because of their ignorance and their resistance; without remorse they have abandoned themselves to lust and the indulgence of every sort of lewd conduct. That is not what you learned when you learned Christ! I am supposing, of course, that he has been preached and taught to you in accord with the truth that is in Jesus: namely, that you must lay aside your former way of life and the old self which deteriorates with illusion and desire, and acquire a fresh, spiritual way of thinking. You must put on that new man created in God's image whose justice and holiness are born of truth. (Eph 4:17-24)

I find it interesting that the Bible says that sexual promiscuity and all the evils associated with it abound when people's hearts and minds are not centered on God. We don't have to look far to see that sexual promiscuity abounds in the world today. The reason is that people are not listening to and being formed by the teachings of the Lord. Today's so-called "liberal" morality is clearly contrary to the word of God. But when our minds are renewed by the Holy Spirit, we begin to think clearly and we become truly liberated in every area of our personality, including our sexuality.

I have singled out sexual sin because the passage from Ephesians deals with it so explicitly. You can add to that vice other modern evils like drug and alcohol abuse, materialism, and political oppression. When our minds as well as our hearts are not centered on the Lord, evil enters in and horrible consequences result. You don't have to look too far in today's world to see the evidence of this drift away from God.

It doesn't have to be that way. God wants his people to have personal lives that are functioning according to his plan. In fact, this is the first place the Lord will work in the life of a disciple. He will show the disciple the areas of sin that need to be repented of and the areas of weakness that need to be strengthened. Then, of course, he will send the power of his Holy Spirit to accomplish these changes.

The passage from Ephesians says that Christians must "acquire a fresh, spiritual way of thinking." This means that the Holy Spirit of Jesus desires to transform our minds. Being a spiritual person does not mean being sweet and vaque, walking around with a pie-in-the-sky mentality. Being spiritual means that we allow the Holy Spirit to form every aspect of our personality including our intellect, our will, our thinking, our attitudes, our point of view, and our philosophy of life—in short, our whole way of approaching reality.

This is a process that takes some time. We will stumble and fall from time to time, but our Master has promised to be with us always. We can expect him to be there whenever we need him.

We develop this kind of Christian mind as we pray, read scripture, and develop relationships with Christians more mature than ourselves. We will discuss each of these in more detail later.

Discipleship is not easy, but it is possible for every Christian. It is the only way to achieve real, lasting joy.

To be a disciple, a Christian must be disciplined. That's why I call this book *The Disciplines of a Disciple.* True disciples must learn how to pray more effectively, how to listen to the Lord more efficiently, how to study scripture and Christian doctrine more profitably, and how to serve God more effectively. All this means living a disciplined life.

That is a tall order. I know how demanding it is because I have lived through years of mistakes and frustration to become the disciple I am today. I am only now realizing how much more I need to learn about discipleship. I still stumble and fall. I am far from being perfect. But I know, despite all the difficulties, that discipleship is possible for every Christian because it is God's work, not our own.

The first disciples were ignorant fishermen in an isolated part of a relatively backward country on the fringe of the great Roman Empire. These fishermen displayed their ignorance again and again even as Jesus Christ, alive in the flesh, was discipling them. Yet in three short years they were transformed into courageous, wise men and women whose apostolic activity built the foundation for a church which changed the course of human history.

God accomplished that great work because the first disciples were willing to allow him to work in their lives. They were willing to learn, to listen, to pray, to struggle, and to suffer. Those five characteristics are all we need to start out on the road of Christian discipleship. We need to be willing to learn from the Master of spiritual teaching. We need to listen to his word and to obey what we hear. We need to pray unceasingly in worship and in petition. We need to be willing to struggle—to make the changes in our lives that the Lord calls for, regardless of how hard they are. Finally, we need to be willing to suffer because no good happens unless we pay a price. Disciples are united with Christ in every way, including his death on the cross, so that with him we can rise to new ways of living and serving on earth and so inherit eternal life.

The actions that I will encourage you to take in the chapters that follow can be compared to the workman who lays forms for a concrete wall. A sturdy and enduring wall is the workman's goal. In our lives, the wall is the life of discipleship already described. Only God can build this wall; he is the one who pours the cement. But concrete is soft and pliable when it comes from the mixer. In order for it to set properly, it needs special forms—sturdy pieces of wood strategically placed to hold the cement in place while it hardens. Putting the forms in place is our job. As we erect the forms, God can pour in the cement. Later, some of the forms will be discarded because they will have served their purpose. Only the work of God will last, and it will last forever.

The process of putting the forms in their proper place is what I call the disciplines of discipleship. The following chapters will discuss some of the forms we need to put in place and the kind of concrete that God will pour into those forms. My hope is that you will slowly read each chapter and reflect on how well the forms are put in place in your life. Then make any changes you need to make and allow God to pour the cement.

Where do we start? By sitting at Jesus' feet just like a young man named James did long ago.

FIVE

Sit at His Feet

JESUS HAD JUST COMPLETED a long journey through Galilee and Syria. He had preached about the kingdom of God and delivered thousands of people from their afflictions. The disciples were tired; so was their Master. But the crowds continued to press upon him. Near the river gathered an immense throng of the sick, the suffering, and the curious. Jesus healed many of them, then he turned, called to his disciples to follow him, and went up a mountainside where the crowd couldn't find him. Jesus didn't say anything for a while. Then he began talking quietly with Peter and John.

James looked at the men sitting around Jesus. "How far we've come from our fishing villages and our customs houses," he thought. "Each of us abandoned everything we know to follow him. I love him more each day, and I think I would die for him if he asked it. But it still seems so odd.

"It is late afternoon now. A year ago at this time I would have been mending nets or cleaning the boat, getting ready for another night of fishing. My father Zebedee is running the business by himself now. He is getting along, but he complains that one old man can't do the work that five men used to do."

James looked at Jesus. He could tell when the Master was ready to teach the disciples. "The miracles are wonderful," he thought. "God is really showing his mercy to his people. But I've seen so many miracles now. It is his teaching that I live for. When he opens our eyes to the words of God, I can hardly contain my joy. I want to run out into the nearest crowd and tell them how great God is, how much love he has shown to us through his holy servant Jesus."

James' mind quieted as Jesus began to speak.

"Blessed are the poor in spirit," he said, "the kingdom of God is theirs.

"Blessed are the sorrowing; they shall be consoled.

"Blessed are the lowly; they shall inherit the land.

"Blessed are they who hunger and thirst for holiness; they shall have their fill.

"Blessed are they who show mercy; mercy shall be theirs.

"Blessed are the single-hearted for they shall see God.

"Blessed are the peacemakers; they shall be called sons of God.

"Blessed are those persecuted for holiness' sake; the kingdom of God is theirs.

"Blessed are you when they insult you and persecute you and utter every kind of slander against you because of me.

"Be glad and rejoice, for your reward is great in heaven; they persecuted the prophets before you in the very same way."

Jesus paused for a few moments, and James and the other disciples reflected on his words.

"Jesus speaks in such strange ways some times," he thought. "We feel so foolish having to ask him what he means. But he is a patient teacher. He's like my father, Zebedee, teaching me how to fish when I was a boy. Jesus patiently explains to us what he means and tells us how to tell others about it."

The apostles were indeed very fortunate to have been taught by Jesus Christ himself. We are fortunate as well, because we have God's word in the scriptures and the teachings of the church to guide us. We can listen to Christ as he speaks through other people and in the stillness of our own hearts.

Scripture study and reflective prayer are important, perhaps the most important of the many supports a disciple needs in order to grow spiritually and to effectively serve the Lord.

The scripture passage from the Gospel of St. Matthew that sets the scene I described earlier reads as follows:

After he had sat down, his disciples gathered around him, and he began to teach them. (Mt 5:1-2)

When we examine that verse closely, we see several important principles for disciples. The phrase "after he had sat down" is important. This phrase is a biblical way of saying "the person who is seated has authority; the person who is seated is one who is recognized as knowing the truth."

When the Bible says, "he had sat down," it refers to the teaching authority of Jesus. His teaching authority is reliable because Jesus is God himself. What he teaches has eternal wisdom and eternal value for us. And that is why being a disciple of Jesus is the most secure reality in the world. When we learn from him, when we pattern our lives after his, when we turn to him with all our needs and in all our joys, we turn to the one who has eternal wisdom and gives eternal life. Each step we take that leads us closer to Christ is a step deeper into his kingdom, a kingdom which lasts forever.

It is important for Christians to know who our teacher is and to make certain we are hearing him correctly. We are taught all day long, by the media, by teachers, by friends, by fads in society. Real life is a constant teacher. But, as we well know, the media and our friends can lead us astray. In many schools today, teachers are actively trying to lead students away from the Lord and his truths.

However, you can't go wrong when you are taught by the Supreme Authority—the one who is the author of all reality. When you are taught by the Lord Jesus Christ himself, you are being taught the truth, and the truth will set you free. We find truth in his teachings, in his word, in the scriptures, and in the living traditions of our church that preserve what God has said to us down through the ages.

As chapter five of Matthew's Gospel shows, one of the most significant things that Jesus did was to form his disciples by teaching. He will teach us, too. To truly be one of his disciples, we must take time every day to sit at his feet so we can be taught by the Master.

Remember your favorite teachers in school. You remember best those who showed a personal interest in you as a person. That is the kind of teacher Jesus is. He teaches us about truth; he teaches us how to live; he tells us what we can and cannot do. But all the while he takes a personal interest in us.

How lucky we Christians are to have a teacher who really knows what he is talking about and who cares for us at the same time. Not only are we given wisdom, but the Wise One himself embraces us, cares for us, and loves us. We not only receive knowledge for our minds, but we receive affirmation and healing love for our hearts.

As a disciple you must take time every day to sit at the Master's feet—to pray and read the scriptures. He cannot do all these wonderful things unless we spend time with him, opening our hearts and lives to him and letting him work in us.

A disciple is also one who imitates the master. Thus a Christian disciple is one who imitates Jesus Christ. St. Matthew's Gospel speaks of this: "The pupil should be glad to become like his teacher. The slave like his master" (Mt 10:24-25).

We should want to imitate Jesus Christ with every dimension of our personalities. We should want to yield every part of our lives to him and allow him to form us to become the person he wants us to be.

I learned this myself one day while in the chapel praying before beginning to film one of my television programs. As I prayed I observed something very interesting occurring in one of the pews. As usual, a group of us were praying very expressively and loudly, and some of us closed our eyes and raised our arms toward heaven in a pose of abandonment to our Lord. On this particular day a man had brought his small son with him. It was very interesting to watch that small boy begin to imitate the style of prayer of the adults around him. Whatever his father did, the boy tried to do also. There was a relationship of imitation between them.

Let me give yet another example. I once took a walk around Manhattan at the time when the rock star Michael Jackson was all the rage. Everywhere I walked in New York I saw young people trying to look and walk and talk like Michael Jackson. Every barber shop seemed to have "you can look like this" posters of Jackson in their windows. Almost every shop had Jackson glasses or Jackson jackets or Jackson shoes for sale.

Young people are taken in by these fads. They imitate the pop heroes of the day. Many times this leads only to trouble, but that is not my point here. My point is that people imitate other people they admire.

The same thing should be true of our relationship with our Father in heaven, the one who made us and who desires to have fellowship with us. We want to imitate him, to be as much like him as we can. The Father sent Jesus into the world to save us, but also to give us teaching that we can learn from and a lifestyle that we can imitate. God wants us to imitate Jesus Christ. He wants us to treat other people the way Jesus did. He wants us to love others as Jesus did. He wants us to serve others as Jesus did. He wants us to pray as Jesus did. He wants us to spread the good news just as Jesus did.

We do this as we become more aware of Jesus' thinking, his attitudes, his lifestyle, even his personality. As we discover these things—by reading the Bible and by daily prayer—something happens to us. We become more Christlike. Jesus is our role model. The more we pattern our lives after the Jesus we see in the gospels, the better disciples we become.

Christians have to be aware, however, of some cautions in this area. It is a sad fact that we tend to forget who our Master is. If we hear a great preacher or join a Christian fellowship with great teachers and impressive ministries, in the months that follow we might be tempted to relegate Jesus Christ to second place.

I am not saying that you should not listen to good preachers and teachers. No Christian can grow properly when isolated from Christian community. I will talk at some length about that later. But we must be clear about who is our master and teacher. It is fine to consider ourselves pupils of a particular Christian teacher or a group of teachers, but they are not our masters. We can have only one master—the Lord himself. He is the one whom we follow. Our goal is to become as much like Jesus as we can.

Jesus' disciples did this throughout the gospels. They followed Jesus, they were always behind him watching and learning from everything he did and said. One time Peter got in front of Jesus and tried to tell the Master not to do something that he knew he had to do. The Lord's response was "get behind me"(Mt 16:23). A disciple is supposed to be behind the Lord, following ever so closely, but always permitting the Lord to take the lead.

There is one supremely important advantage to being led by the Lord Jesus Christ: if you are observing him carefully and correctly, it is hard for you to make big mistakes. If you are led by the world, you will get into trouble. If you allow your emotions to lead you, you will get into trouble. If you are led by what the Bible calls "the flesh"—that is, permitting unredeemed human impulses to be your master—you will always get in trouble.

It is also possible to be led by the Devil. The Bible teaches us that there is an evil being actively at work in the world opposing God's kingdom and trying to confuse his people. In fact, when Jesus told Peter to get behind him, the full remark was, "get behind me, Satan!" Jesus rebuked Peter for doing what the Devil wanted.

So disciples have three potent enemies: the world, the flesh, and the Devil. We can be misled by any of them whenever we take our eyes off the Lord. They lead us away from God's truth and his love. The way to find life is to be led by our Lord Jesus Christ, who always and without fail shows us the way to the Father.

I learned one of the great benefits of discipleship after I became a more committed follower of Jesus Christ in 1969. At that time I was a well-educated, highly motivated, successful Roman Catholic priest. I can honestly say that I loved the Lord. I had dedicated my entire life to him, choosing the celibate priesthood over marriage and family life. You could say that I had said "yes" to being his disciple. But I had done so without fully knowing what that meant. Suddenly, the Lord came into my life in a powerful and dramatic way. Overnight my life and ministry were changed.

It happened on Valentine's Day, 1969. That evening Jesus Christ came personally into my life as he had into the lives of Peter and James and Francis of Assisi. I truly met Christ that night. I looked into his face, and he looked into mine. He gave me his Holy Spirit, and I have not been the same since.

That night I learned that I was called to sit at Christ's feet just as the first disciples did, to listen to his teaching, and to discover life, direction, meaning, and purpose through those teachings. You are too!

How do we do this? By reading and reflecting on the scriptures as often as possible. We also need to study the Bible using reliable Bible study aids.

Why is the Bible so important? In his Second Letter to Timothy St. Paul writes:

All scripture is inspired of God and is useful for teaching—for reproof, correction and training in holiness, so that the man of God may be fully competent and equipped for every good work. (2 Tm 3:16)

The disciple of Jesus Christ takes this passage very seriously and commits himself to study the Bible, the written word of God. A regular Bible study habit is one of the primary ways that a disciple becomes "fully competent and equipped for every good work." The good works Paul writes of are evangelism, Christian service, works of mercy, and every other kind of ministry that bears fruit in the kingdom of God.

A variety of good scripture study methods are available today. Christian magazines often publish Bible study sections each month, and some magazines are devoted exclusively to Bible study. Books, tapes, even board games which describe Bible study techniques are also available. The disciple of Christ should find a method that works well for him or her and follow it without fail.

St. Paul exhorts the disciple to know the scriptures because of their usefulness for teaching, for reproof, for correction, and for training in holiness. At one time or another, every disciple will be called upon to perform one of these important tasks of ministry. You will eventually find yourself in a situation where you will have to teach someone, even if this someone is your own children or friends and neighbors who come over for a cup of coffee.

Similarly, from time to time every disciple will have to correct the misbehavior of someone. It may only be one's children. But it is likely that adult misbehavior, even among your Christian friends, will have to be addressed at one time or another. The scriptures give us guidelines on how to do this:

> If your brother should commit some wrong against you, go and point out his fault, but keep it between the two of you. If he listens to you, you have won your brother over. If he does not listen, summon another, so that every case may stand on the word of two or three witnesses. If he ignores them, refer it to the church. (Mt 18:15-17)

With those words Jesus tells us to correct the wrongdoing of our Christian brothers and sisters. But how do we do it? St. Paul encountered that question and gave this good advice:

> Let everyone speak the truth to his neighbor, for we are members of one another. If you are angry, let it be without sin. The sun must not go down on your wrath. . . . Get rid of all bitterness, all passion and anger, harsh words, slander, and malice of every

kind. In place of these, be kind to one another, mutually forgiving, just as God has forgiven you in Christ. (Eph 4:25-26, 31-32)

St. Paul is not saying to ignore one another's sins. He tells us that the Lord wants us to speak the truth to one another, but to do so without angry or harsh words. "Be kind and forgiving," he says. That's good advice to put into practice when correcting anyone—a child or an adult.

Besides teaching and correction, the scriptures provide us with "training in holiness." Every disciple of the Lord is expected to grow in holiness and to spur other Christians on to holiness. The First Letter of Peter speaks of this call to holiness:

As obedient sons, do not yield to the desires that once shaped you in your ignorance. Rather, become holy yourselves in every aspect of your conduct, after the likeness of the Holy One who called you; remember, Scripture says, "Be holy for I am holy."
(1 Pt 1:14-16)

With those words Peter expresses the need for holiness. But how do we do it? Chapter 12 of the Letter to the Hebrews opens with the two basic actions we need to take:

Since we for our part are surrounded by this cloud of witnesses, let us lay aside every encumbrance of sin which clings to us and persevere in running the race that lies ahead. (Heb 12:1)

The first step in growing in holiness is to "lay aside every encumbrance of sin." Many of us have yet to do that, even though we may have been walking with the Lord for years. We need to make a decision to turn away from all our sins, no matter how large or how small they may be. It doesn't matter if we lack the self-control; God will provide the help we need once we've made the decision to repent, to turn away from sin and towards the new way of life the Lord has for us today.

Perseverance is also a key to growth in holiness. The very next verse gives us the context which keeps us persevering despite human failure and discouragement: "Let us keep our eyes fixed on Jesus, who inspires and perfects our faith" (Heb 12:2).

Keep your eyes on Jesus. Fix your eyes on Jesus. When you hear the call to repentance, it's always joined with the call to faith in Jesus. We don't become holy apart from him. It is Jesus who inspires; it is Jesus who protects; it is Jesus who transforms.

Holiness does not come through gritting your teethand using will power—"I'm going to be holy today." If you focus on your sins and your faults, you could eventually give in to despondency and give up the struggle. Holiness comes through growing, day by day, in commitment to him who is the Author and Finisher of our faith.

Don't mistake me: the word that God is speaking to us about holiness is a hard word. It's no easy, fun thing to become holy. But the word is always said in the context of fixing our eyes on Jesus. That's the context in which we must always hear it.

The Letter to the Hebrews contains much of the practical information we need to go about growing holy. First of all, "Love your fellow Christians always" (Heb 13:1). You don't even have to step out of your house to start doing that. Holiness begins by relating with kindness and patience to those you live with.

The next instruction is: "Do not neglect to show hospitality" (Heb 13:2). What a simple way to grow holy! Especially when we extend our hospitality to more than the nice guests—people from our own background, who cook and eat and think like we do. How about hospitality to those who belong to a different race, or who aren't so easy to get along with, or who are lonely and forgotten?

Another rule for holiness: "Be mindful of prisoners. . . and of the ill-treated" (Heb 13:2). Are you so busy growing holy that you never reach out to others? That's why some individuals and some groups never get anywhere. Be prudent in such service—don't spend so much time in service that you neglect your family or your prayer time. But reach out to others; God's word commands it.

"Let marriage be honored in every way and the marriage bed be kept undefiled" (Heb 13:4). The holiest thing you might do tomorrow is to bring your wife a rose or to cook your husband's favorite dinner. The holiest thing you might do is not criticize and put down one another.

There are many other instructions in scripture about how to grow holy. Every one of them is as simple as these. So let's not complicate the call to holiness. You can start growing holy right where you are, today.

Holiness; patience; fraternal correction; how can you accomplish any of these good things if you don't have a good knowledge of the scriptures? It is impossible! The scriptures are inspired. That means that the word of God breathes with the life of the Father, Son, and Holy Spirit. Its words enlighten our darkness, clear up confusion, fill our minds and hearts with the knowledge and wisdom of God. No disciple can afford to be without it.

As you read and study the word of God, you must be wise and discerning in how you read and understand it. Literalism can be a problem. This is the idea that every single word of the Bible means only what you think it means. It is essential that you use scripture study tools like Bible handbooks written by reputable scripture scholars. (Some are listed at the end of this chapter.)

I also highly recommend that you use a modern translation of the Bible that has footnotes. Read those footnotes as part of your study. These commentaries by scholars do not remove any of the divine Spirit but rather enhance the work of the Holy Spirit as he teaches you.

All scripture study must include a generous period

of time for meditation. When we read the scriptures, we must quiet our minds and let the Spirit of Jesus move in us, guiding us in the way of truth as Jesus promised.

Some Christians believe that the Holy Spirit speaks to mankind only through the scriptures. Most churches, however, hold that the Spirit also speaks to the Christian people as a body. As a Roman Catholic I believe that the Holy Spirit has been active in my church throughout the ages inspiring the popes and the bishops with the help of theologians to interpret God's word in an authentic way. The teachings that the inspired teaching authority of the church have handed on to us are what I refer to as the "teachings of the church." No one can say he or she is a complete disciple of Christ without a good understanding and deeply held faith in the teachings of the church.

I don't intend to discuss any of these teachings. There are plenty of good catechisms that do that. I just want to remind you that Christ founded a church, and that church has a lot to teach you about following the Lord. To benefit from this valuable teaching, you must study it faithfully, believe in it wholeheartedly, and live it unashamedly.

The church also provides us disciples with a context for hearing the Lord more fruitfully in our own lives. The vast resources of the church offer us many opportunities to come together around Jesus in support systems with other disciples. You have to belong to a church community. It means you have to be an active member of that church community, joining together with brothers and sisters in worship, in study, in Christian service, in evangelism, and in fellowship.

Jesus always brought people together. He never intended for us to live our Christian lives alone. Even when he sent the apostles out he sent them out in pairs (Luke, chapters 9 and 10). He intends for us to be in community, and this is what the church is all about. I cannot repeat it strongly enough: a Christian is not a disciple, is not living the way Jesus intends, unless he or she is active in a church body.

The disciple also needs to be devoted to prayer. Right from the beginning of the church Christians have devoted themselves to instruction and prayer (Acts 2:42). Why? Because the only way to learn from the Lord is to spend time with him. We spend time with him by reading the Bible, by contemplation, and by an active prayer life.

In our busy world it is not always easy for disciples to have fruitful prayer lives. But a disciple who cannot pray daily is no disciple at all. Each of us needs to spend time every day with the one who loves us so much that he died that we might live. There is no other way to grow in the knowledge of our beloved Savior. *We must spend time with him daily.*

How? It's really not as hard as it sounds. If you don't have a daily prayer habit right now, begin experimenting. Start by setting aside twenty minutes during a part of the day when your home is relatively quiet. For some people this is in the morning; for others it's the last thing at night. It really doesn't matter *when* you pray, as long as you can be alone and be as isolated as possible from distractions.

The content of your prayer time is, once again, something you should experiment with. What works well for some people may not work well for you. In general I advise that your prayer time begin with a time of verbal praise to God. Praise him out loud, in your own words at first, then move on to exercising the gift of tongues. After that, the Lord will lead you. Your prayer time should include a period of quiet adoration, song, thanksgiving, and prayers of petition for people and situations that require God's mercy and healing.

After you become comfortable with these basics of prayer, you may want to begin meditating on a scripture passage or something you read in a Christian book or heard at a prayer meeting. Meditation is a deeper step into prayer that most disciples take sooner or later.

The most important thing about daily prayer is that you commit yourself to it and that you remain faithful to your commitment. If you find that the time or the place isn't working out, change it. Experiment a little. God will be patient while you are searching for the time and place and style of prayer that works best for you.

Disciples who listen to the Lord soon find that they are ready to experience God's grace in a new way, to engage in ministry. The place to start is doing whatever he says.

Bible Study Helps

1. *Reading Scripture as the Word of God* by George Martin (Servant Books.) A brief but helpful introduction to the Bible.

2. *The Catholic Bible Study Handbook* by Jerome Kodell, OSB (Servant Books.) A popular introduction to the study of the Bible.

3. *God's Word Today* published and edited by George Martin. A monthly magazine which features teaching on Bible themes and a daily reading from the Bible.

4. *Share the Word* published by the Paulist Catholic Evangelization Center. A bimonthly magazine which follows the Sunday liturgical readings in the Catholic Church.

SIX

Do Whatever He Says

PHILIP AND NATHANAEL had been with Jesus only a few days when he told them they were going to attend a wedding feast with him in the town of Cana. The two were excited at the prospect of being seen in public with Jesus, who was held in high esteem because of the things the disciples of John the Baptizer were saying about him. They were also anxious to meet his mother Mary and some of the other disciples whom they did not know.

The two were surprised at how many other guests they knew at the wedding. It seemed like every friend in Galilee had turned out for the affair.

"I had no idea that Jesus knows so many people we also know," Nathanael told Philip. "A lot of these people are here just to see Jesus. They're hoping he'll do something extraordinary."

"That's probably true," Philip said. "But don't forget, there isn't a Jew alive who doesn't love a good party, and wedding feasts are the best parties of all."

"Nathanael, did you notice that the wine we've been served tastes strange?"

"I like it," Nathanael answered. "It's different than the wine we usually drink. I think a wine merchant had it brought in especially for this wedding."

"I didn't say I didn't like it," Philip replied. "I just said that I have never tasted anything like it before."

"Don't bite my head off, Philip," Nathanael said. "I didn't accuse you of anything. Here, let me get you some more wine."

Nathanael motioned to the wine steward who came over to him. "Our glasses are empty, may we have some more wine?"

"I'm sorry," the steward replied, "we are fresh out of wine. We were not expecting so many people at the feast—I didn't realize Jesus would draw such a crowd here.

"Say, aren't you two of his companions? I saw you enter with him."

"Indeed we are," said Philip, his chest swelling with pride. "He invited us to accompany him on his journeys through Galilee. He has been teaching us about the scriptures. We believe that the Holy One has sent him to Israel like he sent the prophets of old."

"Well, I hear that the scribes and the Pharisees are not so excited about the things he says," the steward replied. "I'd be very careful if I were in your shoes."

Unable to get more wine, Philip and Nathanael

made their way across the crowded room to where Jesus was sitting. They noticed that his mother was seated on one side of him and John on the other. They nodded to John, and to Peter and Andrew who were standing off to one side. There were no seats available, so they stood behind Jesus and discussed the wine steward's predicament.

Jesus' mother overheard their conversation. "You say they have no more wine?" she asked Philip. "This must not be. A wedding banquet must have plenty of wine."

Mary turned to Jesus and told him, "They have no more wine."

"Woman," Jesus replied, "how does this concern of yours involve me? My hour has not yet come."

Mary did not answer, but turned to those waiting on the table. "Do whatever he tells you," she said.

Jesus motioned to the six stone water jars along the wall. "Fill those jars with water," he ordered.

The waiters took them out and filled them to the brim with water. Then they carried them back into the room. Few of the wedding guests noticed that it was Jesus who had instructed them to do this.

The wine steward, who had been out of the room when the jars were filled, saw that the jars had been moved away from the wall. He looked inside of one and saw that it was filled with wine. He tasted the wine and then called the groom over. "People usually serve the choice wine first," he said to the groom, "then when the guests have been drinking awhile, a lesser vintage. What you have done is keep the choice wine until now."

Philip and Nathanael were stunned. They knew that the jars had only contained water. They also knew that Jesus was an extraordinary man.

"Could he have changed the water into wine?" Philip asked.

"Of course he did," Nathanael replied. "God has given him great powers. Remember when I first believed in him? He spoke to me in my mind while I was under a fig tree. I hadn't even seen him yet, and he had touched me. At that time he said I would see much greater things than that. And now he changes water into wine. He certainly is the Son of God as he claims."

The other disciples had moved in close to Philip and Nathanael as the jars were being filled with water. They saw what had happened, and they also believed.

Jesus' miracle at Cana served several purposes. One was to prove to his disciples that he was indeed who he claimed to be. They all knew he was extraordinary. They knew that when he spoke of God, he spoke the truth. His teaching worked wonders in their hearts. The miracle at Cana prompted them to remember the stories of the past, when God did mighty deeds among his people. Now, they saw that God was doing mighty things again, through their master Jesus, the Son of God.

The miracle also showed the disciples what great things they could expect from their obedience to Jesus.

If they had any doubts about the wisdom of following him, those doubts certainly disappeared at Cana. Years later, when St. John wrote about the event, he said: "Jesus performed this first of his signs at Cana in Galilee. Thus did he reveal his glory, and his disciples believed in him" (Jn 2:11).

Jesus has also revealed his glory to us, his modern-day disciples who believe in him, who love him, and who want to follow him just as Nathanael and Philip and the other apostles followed him. It only makes sense that if we are going to be his disciples, hear his teaching, and talk with him in prayer, that we must also obey him. Obeying Christ is a necessary step in authentic discipleship.

Mary, the mother of Jesus, showed us the kind of attitude we must have when we hear the word of the Lord. "Do whatever he says," she told the waiters. They obeyed him, and he was able to perform the miracle. Would Jesus have turned water to wine if they had ignored his command? We don't know for sure. But the fact is that Jesus uses men and women as vehicles for his miracles and for his teaching. This vital role in God's kingdom is not limited to the great saints and the leaders of God's people. Jesus intends for every Christian to be a channel of his love and grace and healing. But we can only be such a channel if we listen very carefully to his word and obey it.

The scriptures tell us how we are to obey our Master—fully, joyfully, without complaint. When Jesus says, "Deny your very selves" (Mt 16:24), he means that we are no longer our own boss. He means we have to yield to him, our true master. This doesn't mean that we lose our identities. It means that we *discover* our identities by surrendering totally to our Lord and Master who loves us more than we could ever love ourselves.

When Jesus says, "Follow after me and take up the cross" (Mk 8:38), he means it literally. He wants us to be prepared to give up what we have when he demands this of us, even to the point of giving up our lives for his sake.

We are sometimes tempted to think that the crosses Jesus referred to are only the aches and pains and troubles of daily life. Certainly this is true. But Jesus also means that we are to follow him all the way. He died a horrible death, and he says to us: "You, too, must follow after me and take up your cross, and as I was raised up on the third day, so shall you overcome and be raised up to live with me in eternal glory."

I do not mean to suggest that life's struggles and difficulties are insignificant. They surely are significant, and when we endure them in a prayerful way they can be a source of strength. But the meaning of that passage is literal: as disciples we are obliged to give up whatever it is that Christ calls us to give up.

Christ probably won't call most of us to martyrdom. Our crosses will more likely be some kind of rejection or ridicule, or giving up some of life's pleasures for the sake of the Lord's kingdom. But don't rule martyrdom out. True disciples are prepared even to give up their lives rather than deny Christ and his kingdom.

Such was the case of the Japanese martyrs—a group of young people who were executed in Nagasaki in the 1500s because they refused to deny Jesus Christ and give up their Catholic faith. This is a very inspiring story. Among that group of Japanese martyrs were two teenagers and one eleven-year-old boy named Louis. As he came to the place of execution, young Louis embraced and kissed the cross that had been placed there by the executioners. That little boy was prepared to embrace death rather than deny his faith in Jesus Christ.

As the final preparations were being made to hang him to the cross a wealthy man in the crowd called out to Louis in words like these: "Little boy, you are only eleven years old. This is ridiculous. Leave the Catholic Church, deny this Jesus Christ, come into my house and be my servant. I will take care of you; I will give you everything a boy could want to have. Stop this foolishness and come with me now."

Louis answered the man with words every disciple of Jesus Christ should be willing to say in a similar situation: "Sir, it would better for you to become a Christian and go to the paradise I am going to today."

Because of the courage he displayed in those few short months of his Christian life, Louis is a canonized saint in the Catholic Church today.

The stories of the martyrs throughout Christian history remind us of the seriousness of Christ's call to obedience. None of us knows what the future holds.

Perhaps Christ is calling us to martyrdom. Perhaps he is calling us only to obey him day in and day out as good Christian parents, good members of our church, good participants in our prayer group.

I suspect, however, that God has more in mind than that for each of us. I believe that he is calling each Christian to a special kind of ministry. Perhaps yours is intercessory prayer. We all know how many needs there are for God's mercy and justice in the world today. Intercessors are needed to storm the heavens on behalf of the needs of mankind.

There are many other needs as well. God is calling men and women to bring the word of God to those who don't know him, to bring food and water to those who hunger and thirst, to instruct children and new converts in their faith, to lead (or just faithfully attend) a prayer meeting or Bible study. There are many ways that the Lord calls us to serve his church. He is calling you, his disciple, to one or more of these areas of service. The only way to know your service is through prayer, good discernment, and obedience.

When I become a disciple of the Lord Jesus Christ, I am no longer my own man, as the saying goes. Obviously, the same is true for women. When we make the decision to accept Christ fully into our lives by being his disciples, we lay our own self-interest, our own plans and goals, at his feet. We say, in essence, "I have ideas and plans and goals, but I surrender them to you Lord. I want to do only what you want me to do."

This is, of course, contrary to the wisdom of our

society today. It is truly countercultural. The world says, "Do your own thing; become your own person."

Christians, on the other hand, are called to give up the quest for self and search for Christ instead. We are called not to do our own thing but to do *his* thing. That is the crux of discipleship. Jesus said, "Blest are they who hear the word of God and keep it" (Lk 11:28). It may be uncomfortable sometimes to take that first step in obeying Christ, but the rewards we receive far outweigh our own sacrifices. Sometimes those rewards are a long way off. But they come. We have God's word on it. We know it by experience.

People are very worried about their identity these days. The truth is that you cannot find out who you really are until you lose yourself in Jesus Christ. You cannot discover your real identity, you cannot become the full man or woman you are called to be, until you become a disciple of the Lord Jesus Christ.

In Jesus' time the pagan slaveowners branded their slaves with a hot iron so everyone would know to whom the slave belonged. Christians do a similar thing in baptism. In a ritual action, the sign of the cross is traced on the forehead of the person being baptized. This gesture symbolizes the truth that this new Christian now belongs to Jesus. The gesture lays claim to the person's life on behalf of Jesus Christ. When we are branded with the sign of the cross, we are saying that we are his slaves, his servants, his disciples.

I know many Christian parents who repeat this ritual action each night at bedtime. When praying for their children these parents trace the sign of the cross on the youngsters' foreheads to remind the children and themselves that the child belongs to Jesus Christ. This is a practice that I encourage among disciples of the Lord who have young children. This action teaches them who their Master is and it reminds you of your responsibilities for God's little one whom you are taking care of for the Master.

Obedience is a serious responsibility. Jesus said:

Whoever loves father or mother, son or daughter, more than me is not worthy of me. He who will not take up his cross and come after me is not worthy of me. He who seeks only himself brings himself to ruin, whereas he who brings himself to nought for me discovers who he is (Mt 10:37-39).

As you can plainly see, Jesus demands a great deal from us. As comfortable as we may be in our love for those persons God has placed in our lives—spouse, children, parents, close friends—these relationships cannot be placed ahead of our relationship with the Lord.

Look closely at the passage: "whomever loves father or mother, son or daughter more than me is not worthy of me."

I come from a close and loving Italian-American family. I know what it is like to have a warm relationship with mom and dad. Family life is very strong in the culture I come from, and I love my parents and my brother very much. But the Bible says that my love for Jesus is to be more intense than that. My commitment to him is to have top priority in my life. If my mother or father were to ask me to do something, and I know that the Lord Jesus Christ is clearly calling me to do something else, I must obey Jesus.

Jesus was not trying to cause discord in families when he made this statement. He was trying to show us how vital commitment and obedience are. God's will is often communicated to us through parents, spouses, and friends. For example, if a husband and wife believe God is calling them to some ministry but they neglect their family and a friend points it out to them, they shouldn't quote scripture at the friend. Jesus is probably telling them to pay attention to their children.

We should love our families and our friends. We should lay down our lives for them in every way that we can. But we must keep our priorities straight.

A disciple's top priority is an absolute commitment to Jesus Christ. My commitment is based on a covenant sealed in the blood of the Lord. It is a solemn commitment, but it is also one that places all other relationships in their proper order. The more I walk with Jesus, the more I love, honor, and respect my parents and my brother. In fact, if I am not growing in love for them, if I am not honoring and respecting them, I know that something is wrong in my relationship with the Lord. Love is the principal fruit of discipleship. If I am not growing in love, I am not growing as a disciple.

There are many great examples of people who have obeyed Jesus fully and experienced great growth in love as a result. One of my favorites is St. Francis of Assisi. He was truly a man who gave everything to Jesus, obeyed him, and the world was turned on its ear as a result.

SEVEN

Take Up Your Cross

FRANCIS BERNADONE had been out of circulation for a few months. He had spent time in a Perugian dungeon as a prisoner of war, and then he was laid up by illness. But now he was back parading through the streets of Assisi once again, at the head of a pack of young revelers in a drunken, noisy party.

"Francis has returned," Leonardo said to himself, "and the wine and the jokes flow freely once again. Good old Francis, the life of the party. And he pays the bills too!"

Leonardo had been enjoying the lewd songs the crowd was singing, and it took him a while to notice that Francis was missing. "Where is Bernadone," he wondered. He retraced his steps to find the missing host. He found Francis wondering aimlessly in an alley.

"Bernadone," he cried, "what's going on? Are you sick?"

"No, Leonardo," Francis said. "I'm not sick. I'm praying."

"You've got to be kidding. Praying? That's what old women do. Come on. Let's catch up with the party."

"Go ahead," Francis replied. "I've no interest in parties anymore. I've got a new love in my life."

"What," Leonardo said. "You've got a sweetheart that we don't know about? Let's see her, Bernadone. Are you planning to abandon your friends for her?"

By that time many of the mischief-makers had also retraced their steps and found the two men facing one another.

"Bernadone has a sweetheart," Leonardo said mockingly. "He's going to marry her and leave his friends behind. And on the very night we name him 'king of youth.' Look, he's thrown his scepter into the dirt."

Leonardo picked up the decorated stick that was Francis' scepter. "Your majesty lost his scepter," he said as he handed it to Francis.

Francis held the stick in his hand, looked at every face in the crowd, and proclaimed:

"You're right. I am going to be married. The woman to whom I will give the rest of my life is so rich, so beautiful and so good that none of you has ever seen anyone like her!" With that he fell to his knees and began to pray.

The revellers continued to mock Francis for some time. Then, by ones and twos, they tired of the sport and withdrew.

Who was Francis of Assisi so deeply in love with? Who had turned the head of the young playboy of Assisi? None other than our Lord Jesus Christ. Jesus had come into his heart and promised him a life of fruitful service if he would embrace the cross. The lady Francis was to wed was Lady Poverty, and the life he was to lead was one of radical obedience to Christ.

Biographers tell us that Francis wasn't too concerned with the mocking he had to endure the night he told his friends he was giving up his old way of life. But ridicule hurts us all, and Francis must have been wounded that night. However, whatever pain he endured was slight in comparison with what God called him to in later years.

Francis, whose life has been idealized and romanticized in legends and paintings and movies, endured a great deal of suffering after he became a disciple of Jesus Christ. He was often cold and hungry. When he begged, he was sometimes pelted with rocks and garbage. He was ridiculed by friends and relatives. He was called to minister to some of the most unappealing people in all of Italy and to risk his life sharing the gospel among Muslim warriors. He received the painful stigmata—wounds like those of Jesus Christ in hands and feet. When he died he was in great pain, and the religious order he had founded—the Friars Minor—was being torn apart by factionalism.

Francis endured all these things with heroic peace because he had learned to accept all things from the hands of his Master. He found out that when he suffered Jesus was with him, turning even his sufferings into good fruit for the kingdom of God.

One day not long after his conversion, Francis was riding on horseback when he came upon a leper at a bend in the road. So horrible was the stench and the condition of the man's skin that Francis' first reaction was to turn back. Instead, he dismounted, embraced the poor man, and put some money in his hands. Then he rode off, feeling a happiness of heart he had never experienced before.

God had promised Francis that he would turn bitterness into happiness. He kept his promise. Francis was so caught up in his spiritual euphoria that he rode to a village for lepers nearby, assembled all the residents, and begged their forgiveness for having despised their kind for so many years. Then, according to legend at least, before departing, he kissed each leper on the mouth while giving them money.

That was one of Francis Bernadone's first experiences with the cross. It wasn't his last. Throughout his life he embraced suffering—physical and emotional—for the sake of his Master. He was a complete disciple, willing to accept whatever the Master sent his way in a spirit of joy.

Few of us will be called by the Lord to live the way St. Francis did. His was a special calling, and to him the Lord gave special graces. But, for each of us, discipleship often involves hardship, sacrifice, disappointment, and suffering. The apostles experienced it—how do you suppose St. John felt at the foot of Jesus' cross? Francis experienced it. So do you and I.

Why is this so? Jesus said:

> If a man wishes to come after me, he must deny his very self, take up his cross and begin to follow in my footsteps. Whoever would save his life will lose it. But whoever loses his life for my sake will find it. What profit would a man show if he were to gain the whole world and destroy himself in the process? (Mt 16:24-26)

You and I are called to be disciples. Jesus says to us, very personally, that if we really wish to follow him, we must deny our very selves, take up our crosses, and begin to follow in his footsteps. If we lose our lives for his sake, we gain life indeed!

Not so long ago a young woman in Germany made that kind of commitment. She gave up everything to follow Christ, she suffered greatly, but the fruit of the Holy Spirit flowed from her. Her name is Edith Stein.

On August 9, 1942, Edith Stein was stripped naked, marched into a gas chamber at Auschwitz and killed. What makes her extraordinary is that she was a Carmelite nun. She could have escaped but chose not to.

When Edith Stein told her family that she had been baptized a Catholic, her mother burst into tears. A hardworking widow, Mrs. Stein couldn't understand how her daughter could abandon the Jewish values she had been been brought up with.

"I have nothing against Christ," Mrs. Stein told Edith several years later. "It is possible that he was a very good man. But why did he have to make himself God?"

Edith did not view her conversion as a repudiation of anything. Nor was she drawn to Christianity because Jesus was a good man. This brilliant young woman, a celebrated intellectual giant, saw her commitment to Jesus Christ as the climax of a long search for truth. It was the cross of Jesus Christ that helped her find that truth.

When writing of the moment of her conversion, Edith said, "I saw the redemptive suffering of Christ overcoming death. This was the moment when my unbelief broke down and Christ appeared to me in the mystery of the cross."

The cross was the central factor in Edith's spirituality from that moment on. When she entered the Carmelite Order, she took the name Sister Teresa Benedicta of the Cross. Then she watched in horror as anti-Jewish sentiment grew in Nazi Germany and the cross of persecution descended on her people.

Sister Teresa left Germany in an effort to shield her monastery from problems with the Gestapo. She went first to a monastery in Holland, then applied for permission to transfer to a monastery in Switzerland where she would be free of the Nazis. But she and her sister Rosa, who had also converted to Catholicism, were arrested before the transfer could be completed.

The sisters were sent to a holding camp. Many of the people in the camp were Catholic priests and nuns who had been arrested for aiding Jews. Each day they gathered for prayer and then ministered to the other detainees. One man, a Dutch employee of the camp, was so moved by Sister Teresa's devotion to the Lord and to her fellow prisoners that he offered to arrange for her freedom. She refused, believing that Jesus Christ wanted her to stay until the bitter end to offer hope and encouragement to all she could. A few days later she was shipped to Auschwitz and executed.

Edith Stein stands as a shining modern example of the kind of attitude Christian disciples have held through the ages. The disciple is able to obey Christ, no matter the cost, because the power of his cross and resurrection is always available.

Edith also discovered how to learn from suffering. We need to learn this early in our training in discipleship. Every person experiences many kinds of suffering, from the relatively small difficulties of daily living to those traumatic experiences such as accidents, disease, and death. Suffering is a part of life, a consequence of humanity's fall from grace. No one can escape it. The holiest and most spiritual Christians experience suffering. How we respond to it is one of the key tests of spiritual maturity, of growth as a disciple of Jesus Christ.

The Lord wants to use all the difficult circumstances

of life to teach us how to be better disciples. No one is more capable of teaching this to us than our Master Jesus Christ who experienced some of the worst kinds of difficulties any man has ever had to face. He learned many things by his obedience and by his suffering, and he wants us to learn the same way.

Scripture teaches this very clearly:

> In the days when he was in the flesh he offered prayers and supplications with loud cries and tears to God who was able to save him from death, and he was heard because of his reverence. Son though he was, he learned obedience from what he suffered. And when perfected, he became the source of eternal salvation for all who obey him. (Heb 5:7-9)

Jesus' sufferings put him in the right place before God. He accepted, even embraced, suffering and death. By doing so he won salvation for us.

When you belong to Jesus Christ, you belong to someone who has been through it all. There isn't a pain, a suffering, or a difficulty of any kind that you can possibly experience that the Lord Jesus Christ himself cannot understand. Because of his full humanity, he has been there. He plunged into the human condition. He knows it in its depth and its darkness.

Because we belong to someone who understands our sufferings, we can take those sufferings and join them with the crucified and risen One. Yes, we ask for healing. Yes, we ask for relief from our suffering. Yes, we ask for the burdens to be lifted—and often they are. But at other times God does not answer our prayer right away or in the way we expect him to answer. Christians suffer. People die. Holy, believing men and women of God experience diseases. But our victory lies in the fact that we do not allow any kind of suffering to cause us to lose our hope and our faith in Christ Jesus our Lord. We embrace the crucified and risen One, and we take that pain and offer it to him. We unite our sufferings with his sufferings on the cross even as we are asking for healing. In that way we are victorious because we are plugging into his victory.

I have practiced this in my own life, and I know many others who do also. It is something that Catholics once called "offering it up." When I do this I do not make it a casual thing. I offer a conscious prayer, saying something like this:

"Lord, I don't want to suffer like this. I wish you would take this difficulty away from me. But if it is your will that I suffer, then I want to unite it with the suffering of Jesus. I open my heart and mind to whatever it is you want me to learn from this situation. Help me to understand."

My experience, and that of many other Christians whom I have had the privilege of sharing trials with, is that we become stronger as disciples. This can only happen when we recognize that our basic call is to a faith relationship with Jesus Christ. We hold onto that even if our sufferings increase, even if our prayers do not seem to be answered right away and as we expect them to be answered.

Suffering can have other beneficial effects. When we accept our sufferings, embrace them, and offer them to the Lord we grow in courage, in strength of spirit, in character.

This is spoken of in the First Letter of Peter:

When a man can suffer injustice and endure hardship through his awareness of God's presence, this is the work of God in him. If you do wrong and get beaten for it, what credit can you claim? But if you put up with suffering for doing what is right, this is acceptable in God's eyes. It was for this you were called, since Christ suffered for you in just this way and left you an example, to have you follow in his footsteps. (1 Pt 2:19-21)

This section of the epistle was written to Christian slaves, encouraging them to withstand the abuse they often received at the hands of their masters. It applies also to we who suffer abuse today. But it can also apply to those of us who suffer from sickness or poverty or other kinds of distress. "If you put up with suffering," the epistle says, and choose to stay free of sin (see verse 23), you are pleasing God.

I know about a religious sister in a city in the Midwest whose life exemplifies this very thing. She has been bedridden for about twenty years with a painful disease that is incurable but also not fatal. She cannot move herself or feed herself. Everytime she is moved to have the bed linens changed, she loses large patches of skin. These exposed patches are painful for days.

This sister has been prayed with for healing many times, yet her disease goes on unchecked. Why? Because God wants her to be a special kind of spiritual warrior. She prays for hours each day for a long list of special needs of God's people today. Heading her list are the needs of modern families, which are under so much strain and attack from the forces of darkness. Her friends believe that sister's prayers have been responsible for the success of several important Christian family ministries in her area.

This sister found out that if she united her sufferings with those of Christ, he could use them to build up his people. Many of us will be called to do the same kind of thing, although probably not to the degree that sister has been called.

Suffering also is sometimes a test that comes to us from God to make sure that our faith is a relationship with him and not a relationship with our emotions. Our faith is not to be based on feelings or logic. We have faith in a person—Jesus Christ. Our faith is a relationship with him and a commitment to him. During those times of trial and suffering when we can say, "I love you, Jesus Christ, no matter what," we know our faith is strong and we know that even our pain and sufferings will work out for the good. We have assurance for all these things. We can become stronger disciples when we know how to cope with suffering even as we ask the Lord to heal us.

There are many places in scripture that we can turn to for comfort and reassurance at such times. One of my favorites is the following from the Epistle to the Romans:

> Who will separate us from the love of Christ? Trial, or distress, or persecution, or hunger, or nakedness, or danger, or the sword? ... I am certain that neither death nor life, neither angels nor principalities, neither the present nor the future, nor powers, neither height nor depth nor any other creature, will be able to separate us from the love of God that comes to us in Christ Jesus, our Lord."
>
> (Rom 8:35-39)

EIGHT

Gathering of Disciples

"WE SHOULD HURRY BACK to our brothers, John," Peter said after they had been dismissed by the Sanhedrin. "They will be concerned about us."

John and Peter had been summoned to account for themselves before the high priests. Their continuing proclamation of the resurrection of Jesus had angered the Jewish leaders. But their healing of the lame man at the Beautiful Gate had really gotten them in trouble. The miracle was being talked about all over Jerusalem, and the priests wanted the talk stopped.

Peter and John would not back down. Peter had boldly proclaimed the truth of Jesus Christ before the Sanhedrin and pointed to the healing of the man as proof of the power of the gospel. They were dismissed with a warning not to speak the name of Jesus in public again. They could not agree to this, but they were dismissed anyway.

Peter and John walked quickly back to the place where the other disciples were anxiously waiting for them.

"We are safe," Peter said when they had been admitted to the house.

He and John then related all that had happened. Their friends were especially pleased to hear that they had the opportunity to proclaim the gospel to the leaders of the people.

After hearing the story, the believers fell to their knees, worshipping the Lord and gave him thanks.

"O Lord, look at the threats they are leveling against us," they prayed. "Grant to your servants, even as they speak your words, complete assurance by stretching forth your hand in cures and signs and wonders to be worked in the name of Jesus, your holy Servant."

While they were still praying, God answered their petitions in a most remarkable way. The Holy Spirit descended anew on each disciple there, and the house shook as if from a mighty earthquake. After the prayers, the apostles discussed how to continue to proclaim the good news of Jesus Christ.

Peter went off to pray to his beloved Master for a time. As he prayed, he reflected on all that was happening.

"Our small band is growing, Lord. You sent the Holy Spirit just as you promised, and we have come a long, long way since the day of Pentecost. Then we numbered only a few dozen. Now there are thousands of believers in Jerusalem and throughout Judea and Galilee.

"You are building us into a people, Lord Jesus. A people who follow your way to salvation. Where it will all lead, I do not know. But I thank you, Lord, for visiting your people with power so that we can proclaim your salvation."

Peter, the man Jesus chose to lead his church during its first years, could not imagine how much larger the body of Christian people would soon become. He had not suffered much as yet for the sake of the gospel. The first martyr had yet to shed his blood. But Jesus was active, building his people into what Peter would later describe as "'a chosen race, a royal priesthood, a holy nation, a people he claims for his own to proclaim the glorious works' of the One who called you from darkness into his marvelous light" (1 Pt 2:9).

We usually date the founding of the church from the day of Pentecost, when the Lord sent the Holy Spirit in power upon his apostles. On that day the disciples began to exercise the mission Jesus had called them for. But Jesus had been preparing them for some time for that day. A passage we have discussed before throughout this book, way back in the beginning of St. Matthew's Gospel, says the following: "After he [Jesus] had sat down his disciples gathered around him" (Mt 5:1).

Jesus gathered his disciples around him so that he could teach them and form them. We too need to sit at his feet, alone, as individuals with our own unique relationship with the Lord. But we also need to gather around him with other disciples. In the midst of such a gathering we recognize that he is present, that he desires to teach us through his word, that he desires to form us into a people who can support one another and serve him in unity, strength, and power. This is a lesson the apostolic church learned very early. We need to learn it too.

There is a wise expression Christian teachers sometimes use that applies here: "Jesus didn't write a book; he founded a church."

What this means is that Jesus did not map out a specific strategy for his disciples. He told them what their objectives were—to make disciples of all nations, baptizing them and teaching them. He also told the disciples that they would have the Holy Spirit ever with them leading them into all truth. These disciples and their successors under the inspiration of the Holy Spirit and using the authority given them by Jesus, developed the building blocks for the growth of individual Christians as part of the church.

What are those building blocks? Christians are to join together in a body of believers for mutual spiritual edification, for daily support, and for united service in the name of Christ to the world around them.

Any disciple who is not part of such a community needs to become part of one. We all need to belong to a church community where we worship, fellowship, and serve with other believers.

Christians simply cannot do without the church. It not only is a psychological and social need, but it is a divine command. Jesus established a church. Peter and

Paul and the other apostles planted that church in soil around the world. They did not want people to become isolated Christians united only by similar beliefs. Their desire, which Jesus himself had planted in their hearts, was that men and women join together in common faith, common worship, and a sharing of daily life. Therefore, as obedient disciples ever ready to follow our Master, we are faithful, active members of our church. The Letter to the Hebrews says it so well! "We should not absent ourselves from the assembly, as some do, but encourage one another" (Heb 10:25).

After those first disciples experienced "being baptized with the Holy Spirit" they entered into a lifestyle described in Acts 2:42:

> They devoted themselves to the apostle's instruction and the communal life, to the breaking of bread and the prayers.

I have found that the liturgy of the Church is a most important "discipline of discipleship." As a Roman Catholic Christian I give top priority to the "apostolic instruction" which comes through the daily assigned scripture readings of liturgy, both the Liturgy of the Word and those readings found in the Liturgy of the Hours. I believe the Lord instructs and forms us through the liturgical cycle of readings and the liturgical year, from Advent through the Solemnity of Christ the King. I want to encourage my readers who belong to liturgical Christian churches to value their liturgical customs.

Jesus speaks to us through the sacred liturgy. The liturgy of the Church provides a framework within which we can experience "discipling." I look upon the liturgy as an organized program of personal and communal formation over the period of a year. Liturgical spirituality is a contemporary way of devoting oneself "to the breaking of bread and the prayers." Without such a framework one is left to personal spontaneity in one's prayer life. In fact what will happen is that you will develop your own "ritual" or "paraliturgy" in terms of your personal prayer life. Why not submit to the richness of the church's official prayer life or at least integrate your personal spontaneity within the framework of what is established for us by church elders?

Jesus disciples us in a most excellent and central way through the Eucharist. As a Catholic Christian I give great emphasis to the tradition of the "breaking of bread" as witnessed to in Paul's Letter to the Church in Corinth:

> I received from the Lord what I handed on to you, namely, that the Lord Jesus on the night in which he was betrayed took bread, and after he had given thanks, broke it and said, "This is my body, which is for you. Do this in remembrance of me." In the same way, after the supper, he took the cup, saying, "This cup is the new covenant in my blood. Do this, whenever you drink it, in remembrance of me." Every

time then you eat this bread and drink this cup, you proclaim the death of the Lord until he comes!
(1 Cor 11:23-26)

In chapter ten of the same letter Paul writes:

Is not the cup of blessing we bless a sharing in the blood of Christ? And is not the bread we break a sharing in the body of Christ? Because the loaf of bread is one, we, many though we are, are one body, for we all partake of the one loaf. (1 Cor 10:16-17)

Everytime we celebrate the Eucharist and partake of Holy Communion we are engaged in the most important act of worship a disciple of Jesus' can be about. Jesus comes to us in that sacred meal and "disciples" us. He heals, strengthens, and delivers us from evil. He speaks words of instruction and encouragement. He molds, forms, corrects, edifies, in short, acts upon our personhood in a relationship of profound covenant love. Through each Eucharist he also seeks to unite his body, the church, and bring salvation to the whole world.

One good exercise I recommend for every Christian, Catholic or otherwise, is to study carefully the official prayer books of your church. What a church prays, a church also believes. When I want to understand better the authentic beliefs of the Catholic Church I study carefully the official liturgical prayers of the church. I am convinced that they are most important disciplines of discipleship. How grateful I am to Father Bertrand

Fay of the diocese of Albany, New York, who planted within me years ago a love for the liturgy of the Church.

Quite often, after Mass, I will go to a private place, alone and just spend fifteen minutes or so thanking the Lord for his gift of "the breaking of bread." Then I will listen quietly, expecting him to talk to me. After all, I am his disciple and I know he has something personal to say to me. The moments after Communion are the most precious ones in my ongoing discipling relationship with the Lord. I keep a notebook handy and write down what I believe he is saying to me. One can accumulate very profound instructions over the course of days. My awareness of his words is not always clear and accurate, but I trust him and I know he loves me even when I am distracted and find it hard to listen. You see, the disciple can come to the Master just as he is. Sometimes I come very weak and tired, with a mind filled with many concerns. But I come, and encourage you to do the same especially through the "bread of life and the cup fo salvation."

> Lord, to whom shall we go? You have the words of eternal life. (Jn 6:68)

> The man who feeds on my flesh and drinks my blood remains in me, and I in him. (Jn 6:56)

> Lord Jesus Christ, Son of the living God, by the will of the Father and the work of the Holy Spirit your death brought life to the world. By your holy body

and blood free me from all my sins, and from every evil. Keep me faithful to your teaching, and never let me be parted from you. (Prayer of priest before Holy Communion—Roman Missal)

One comment I hear a lot from people is that they "are not being fed" in the church they belong to. In fact, apparently quite a few people leave their own church for another because of the quality of the sermons or the degree of fellowship or friendliness they experience. It is truly sad that Christians do not experience good teaching and wholesome fellowship in their own church. But I believe it is a tragic mistake to leave a spiritual home simply on the basis of a perception of unfulfilled spiritual or emotional needs. A basic biblical principle of Christian life applies here: it is not what we receive that makes the church grow and prosper; rather, it is what we *give*.

People who think their church is not feeding them sufficiently simply have to act like adults and take responsibility for feeding themselves. We don't have to "be fed" all the time; sometimes we have to feed ourselves.

After a dry church service the best thing to do is to sit down with your Bible and turn to the Lord in prayer. If you open your heart to God, he certainly will not bore you. He will feed you with the bread of life, and then you can gather with other disciples and study what he teaches you. What an antidote to a dry church community!

As they grow as disciples, many people become equipped to counteract dryness in their church. As they attain a certain level of spiritual maturity and can demonstrate it to their pastors, they are often called upon to provide education and inspiration for others in a Christian education course or another church program. Maybe this is God's plan for you, too.

Another objection I often hear about the church comes from people who are unwilling to invest the time necessary to grow to spiritual maturity in their own church. They look elsewhere for someone who will do it for them and tell them what they want to hear. They make excuses like, "I'm not intelligent enough to understand when God is teaching me."

We read about people like this in the scriptures. Peter, the one Jesus chose to lead the rest of his disciples, demonstrated some of the attributes of a thick-head. Peter and his colleagues were not very well educated. They were simple fishermen. The women who followed Jesus were simple women. Yet our Lord Jesus Christ was able to teach them enough to change the course of human history.

Our Lord does not speak just to the educated, to the intelligent, or to others who are held in high esteem in the world. He desires to speak simply and clearly and lovingly to every man, woman, and child on the face of the earth. He does not look at your IQ before he encourages you to get involved in Bible study. He does not care what your achievement tests in school revealed about your ability to learn before he speaks to you in the quiet of your heart. He loves you so much that he wants you to know the truth that will save you! He wants you to think clearly so you will be able to respond to his love when he makes it known. He wants you to be educated in spiritual ways so that he can speak to you through his Holy Spirit, even during those times when you stumble through the word of God.

You certainly *will* stumble through the word of God at times. There will be passages you do not understand or which seem to contradict other passages you have read. There will be times when your prayer life seems barren. There will be times when your church community seems oppressive and fellowship seems as attractive as having your teeth pulled out. But these difficult times are usually short-lived. They are part of the price we pay for being human. And God can and will use them, just as he uses every other circumstance in our lives, to teach us.

Besides being active members of the church disciples also need to belong to a smaller body of Christians with whom we can share our hopes and sorrows and joys intimately. Hopefully, this kind of sharing group can exist within the structure of one's church community. When that isn't possible, the individual has to go ahead and organize one in the home.

Such a sharing group may be as small as two or three other people. Who among us does not know two or three other earnest Christians we can gather with for prayer, fellowship, service, and study? Such a Christian support system is absolutely vital.

If you do not have such a support system, you should ask God to give you one. Ask him to show you what to do. He will do one of two things: either send you those brothers and sisters who you can become community with, or lead you to a group that already exists.

Don't forget these simple truths: as disciples we are not in a relationship with a book, no matter how sacred it may be, or with a church, no matter how wonderful it may be. We are in a relationship with a person. Our faith is not some intellectualized system of knowledge, it is a loving relationship with the living God. When you come upon a rough spot in a relationship with a pastor or a friend, when you come upon something in scripture or the teaching of the church that you don't understand, take it to the Lord. Because you are a disciple, you can go to him in a direct way and say, "Lord, help me. Lord, teach me." And you know what? He will!

When I became pastor of a small parish in upstate New York, I discovered that Catholics rarely spoke about their spiritual experiences. I started to encourage the people to talk about what God had been doing in their lives. The response was simply amazing. Most of the elderly men and women in the parish had never told anyone about their experience of God in their lives. But when they began to talk about these experiences they could see that God had indeed been at work, just as he had in the lives of Christians—ordinary people as well as saints—down through the ages.

I did not bring any new insight into their lives. God had been active. In fact, when I spoke from the pulpit some of the older people said things like, "Thank God somebody is finally telling us that. I heard that from the Lord a long time ago."

Jesus Christ is always active. When we sit at his feet, in private prayer and meditation and in community prayer and study, we learn his wisdom for living. Jesus Christ wants you to learn about him, to know him, to love him, to care for him. Then, as you sit at his feet and gather with others in his name, he not only teaches, but he cares for you, he shepherds you, he loves you. He fills you up with spiritual things so that you can become the kind of man or woman that he wants you to be.

We need to do all this within a church community. I live out my Christian life as a disciple within the fellowship of the Roman Catholic Church. I enjoy all of the sacraments and disciplines and authority of the church. This is all part of being discipled: the church influences my thinking, my attitudes, my approach to morality, the way I approach the scriptures. The church has a rich life of liturgy and spirituality. Through each of these the Lord himself disciples me.

As a Catholic I believe that when I hear the voice of my bishops teaching in union with the Holy Father, when I hear the instruction of the Holy Father and the teachings of the great church councils (especially Vatican II because it speaks to our generation), I am hearing the voice of the Lord Jesus Christ. Why is this so? Jesus himself said it when he told the disciples "He who hears you hears me" (Lk 10:16).

I can hear the voice of the Lord as his Spirit speaks to

me in the privacy of my room. I can study the Bible and be edified by its timeless message of truth. I am instructed and built up and blessed by all kinds of devotions. However, I do all that in the context of belonging to the church—the body of Christ. I am discipled along with the pastors, teachers, prophets, and evangelists of the church, with the bishops and pope and all the other authorities that the Lord has placed within the church as part of his plan of discipling me.

Being fully within the church means that I am fully involved in the sacramental life of the church, that I am fully docile to the authority of the church, that I fully accept of the disciplines of the church, that my heart and mind and soul are set on the liturgies and prayer life of the church, that my resources and my talents are put to the service of the church. Through the giving and the receiving of church life, I am being discipled by my Lord Jesus Christ. Once we are firmly placed in Christ's body, we need to go out and spread the gospel. Let's start by recalling a journey taken by a young man named Mark.

NINE

Make Disciples
of All Nations

M ARK WATCHED THE WAVES crash against the prow
of the ship. It was now six days since he had left
Paul and Barnabas preaching in the city of Perga. He
was anxious to return to Jerusalem, but he couldn't
overcome the feeling that he was missing something.
He had enjoyed the incredible excitement that always
accompanied Paul's first visit to a city where the gospel
of Christ was unknown.

"Paul has a knack for creating a stir wherever he
goes," the young man thought. "He gets the attention
of the synagogue leaders and the Roman officials as
well. And the Lord seems to use everything he does to
bring people to believe in the Christ."

Mark strolled about the deck and strained his eyes
for any sight of land. In the distance he thought he

could make out some low hills. "We are getting close to port," he thought. "I'll be in Jerusalem in a few days. I wonder what the Lord has in store for me there."

Mark was a young Jew who had embraced the gospel, partly through the influence of his cousin Barnabas. He had traveled with Paul and Barnabas as "servant," recently, to several towns on the island of Cyprus. Mark later became something of a missionary himself, both in association with Peter, who calls him "my son" (1 Pt 5:13) and in his own right as the first disciple to write a gospel.

Like many of the men in the first Christian community in Jerusalem, Mark dedicated his life to evangelism because he knew that faith in Jesus Christ means salvation to all who embrace him, as well as life to the full, freedom and joy, during this life on earth. Mark was a true disciple of the Master because he opened his life to others by sharing the good news of what Jesus had done for him. Like Mark, we should also be disciples who are dedicated to evangelism.

Few of us will be called to preach the gospel on foreign shores like Mark did. The most evangelistic writing we ever do will probably be letters to our friends. But we are called to embrace every opportunity to communicate the gospel to people around us for our sake as well as for their own. The disciple grows in his experience of new life as he goes out into life's highways and byways seeking out guests for the master's victory banquet.

"Full authority has been given to me both in heaven and on earth. Go therefore and make disciples of all the nations" (Mt 28:19).

Jesus speaks those words to us also. Our primary calling as disciples, the major activity of our new life in Christ, is to share the good news we have discovered with every man, woman, and child we can.

There are many different ways to evangelize. Some people stand on street corners and preach. Some proclaim the gospel in huge sports arenas. Others stand before television cameras. Others seek out situations where they can present the gospel message to complete strangers, like witnessing to someone during an airplane ride.

Probably the most common and most natural kind of evangelism is speaking of Christ, of his mercy and his love, to our relatives, our friends, our neighbors, and anyone else the Lord places in our lives.

Pope Paul VI spoke of this in his letter on evangelization:

> Above all the gospel must be proclaimed by witness. Take a Christian or a handful of Christians who, in the midst of their own community, show their capacity for understanding and acceptance, their sharing of life and destiny with other people, their solidarity with the efforts of all for whatever is noble and good. Let us suppose that, in addition, they radiate in an altogether simple and unaffected way their faith in values that go beyond current

values, and their hope in something that is not seen and that one would not dare to imagine. Through this wordless witness these Christians stir up irresistible questions in the hearts of those who see how they live: Why are they like this? Why do they live in this way? What or who is it that inspires them? Why are they in our midst? Such a witness is already a silent proclamation of the good news and a very powerful and an effective one. Here we have an initial act of evangelization. . . .

All Christians are called to this witness, and in this way they can be real evangelizers.

These words of the Holy Father remind us of the wisdom found in the First Letter of Peter: "Should anyone ask you the reason for this hope of yours, be ever ready to reply" (1 Pt 3:15).

The Holy Father and the scripture tell us that the most basic way we evangelize is by living a good Christian life and telling others explicitly about the Lord when they ask us why we are different than others. If we are truly living a daily life of commitment to discipleship, we will be different, and people will notice it. We will have hope; we will be kind and polite; we will always stand up for the truth and for justice. All this will be noticed.

A man who did this is my friend Bill, a college professor. When Bill took a job teaching history at a state university, he decided that he would always be open about his Christian faith with his students and his fellow teachers.

He didn't have to wait very long for an opportunity to share about Jesus Christ.

The first day of classes a student approached Bill after class and told him he was in trouble. The young man had just returned to college after dropping out for a few semesters. He had had a drug problem and had managed to overcome it, but he needed a lot of support to get his life back on track again. He asked Bill for suggestions on ways to study so that he could do well in his academic work.

Bill did share some study ideas with the young man. Then he began to share a little about his faith in Christ. When the young man told him he would like to hear more, Bill invited him home for dinner. The student came and was so impressed with Bill and his family, that he decided to commit his life to Christ. He took some religious instructions, joined the campus parish, and began making new friends, Christian friends. Today that man is a successful attorney, a husband and father of a strong Christian family, a leader in his parish and a key man in an evangelistic program in his city.

Not all of Bill's students responded like this one did. But many students have heard the gospel simply because of Bill's decision to be open about his faith and to answer questions about his faith directly.

Many Christians tend to beat around the bush when

someone asks them questions or pays them a compliment about their family or their lifestyle. This is not acceptable for a disciple. "Be ever ready to respond," the Letter of Peter advises us. "All Christians are called to this witness," adds Pope Paul VI.

There are many creative ways to witness by the example of our daily lives. Christian homemakers do it by inviting neighborhood women into their homes for coffee and a chat. Men and women alike witness in their workplaces by being honest, hardworking, and generous towards fellow workers and customers. Christian young people witness for Christ by refusing to bow to peer pressure when immoral activities are suggested by companions.

Regardless of how effective evangelism by the witness of our daily lives may be, we are all called to evangelize actively. Consider what Pope Paul wrote in the section of his letter on evangelism which immediately follows the section on witness:

Even the finest witness will prove ineffective in the long run if it is not explained, justified—what Peter called always having "your answer ready for people who ask you the reason for the hope that you all have" [1 Pt 3:15]—and made explicit by a clear and unequivocal proclamation of the Lord Jesus. The Good News proclaimed by the witness of life sooner or later has to be proclaimed by the word of life. There is no true evangelization if the name, the teaching, the life, the promises, the kingdom and the mystery of Jesus of Nazareth, the Son of God are not proclaimed.

How you evangelize is not as important as doing what the Lord wants you to do—that is, to evangelize. Don't let timidity or fear or any other obstacle stand in the way. We have a command from our Master. Obey it.

We must also think of the salvation of the person at stake. Do we want anyone we know, anyone we meet, to run the risk of not entering into the joys of eternal life with Christ? Is there anyone you know whom you don't want to see in heaven? Of course not! So, be open to evangelizing.

There are many ways that we can evangelize during the course of our daily lives. I sum them up in four words: care, prayer, share, and dare.

We *care* about people when we approach them with love and concern. We demonstrate love by our attitudes and behavior. A genuine love for the other person rises from our hearts, which are in touch with Jesus through prayer.

We exhibit love and concern in our posture, our tone of voice, our manner. We also care for persons we are evangelizing by being willing to support them in practical ways: giving them rides to church or prayer meetings; offering books to read; watching their children; inviting them into our homes for meals and socializing. True care, which is a fruit of personal prayer, is a key ingredient in evangelization.

What the disciples spoke to Jesus—"Everybody is looking for you!" (Mk 1:37)—is true. Many people are not consciously aware that they are looking for Jesus, but they are looking for *something*. Each person comes into the world with an empty space within, a space made only for God. They can try to fill that space with everything but God, but sooner or later they realize that the things of earth don't meet the need. These are prime times for evangelism—times of pain and suffering, times of doubt and confusion, moments of unexplainable happiness. When a Christian, supported by prayer, is there to care at these times, many people give their lives to Jesus Christ.

An important part of caring for another is to listen to that person. Caring by listening is also an important part of the evangelization process because when we listen to a person we are more aware of the right moment to share about our relationship with Christ.

We also need to pray every day for those we have had the privilege of witnessing to. Whoever and wherever they are, no matter how many there are, pray for them! Intercede in their behalf. Intercede with God for evangelism and evangelists in general. St. Paul, one of the greatest Christian evangelists, begged the young Christian community in Ephesus to support his ministry with their prayers:

Pray for me that God may put his word on my lips, that I may courageously make known the mystery of the gospel—that mystery for which I am an ambassador in chains. Pray that I may have courage to proclaim it as I ought. (Eph 6:19-20)

Disciples of Christ should pray that God will bless the evangelists he has raised up. We should pray that he will raise up more lay evangelists. We should pray for those who have been ordained to the official ministry of the church—our pastors and bishops. Pray for them that God will put his word on their lips and that they would courageously make known the full truth of the gospel.

You *share* Christ when you tell someone what Christ has done for you. It may take the form of sharing how you solved a problem similar to theirs or how you found the strength to cope with life. If you feel moved to offer your personal testimony or share about your personal faith life or your prayer life, I recommend that you "ask permission" first. This allows the other person to choose freely to be in a receptive mode. No use telling someone about your faith in Jesus Christ if he is not going to listen. I would say something like: "I appreciate what you have been telling me. May I ask you something? May I share with you how my life has been changed; how I have discovered how real Jesus Christ is and how I have found a new life in him?"

With the person's permission, you can begin to give your personal testimony. Do not talk in the abstract. Give your personal story, not a theological treatise. Friendly, caring conversation is in order. Your objective should be to motivate the other person to want to initiate a similar relationship with Jesus. When such motivation is aroused, you may follow through in a number of ways.

The most direct way of helping someone enter into a personal relationship with Jesus is to lead him or her in a prayer that expresses their desire.

Other ways of helping the person begin such a relationship with Jesus is to bring them to a prayer meeting or to a Christian leader you know who can help them.

As a Catholic evangelist I am also concerned that any Catholics I evangelize be directed toward making a good sacramental confession. I believe God wants the evangelization of Catholics to result in a sacramental life, especially the sacraments of baptism, confirmation, reconciliation (confession), and Eucharist.

I also strongly recommend that each evangelizer have at his or her disposal other resources to complete the process of evangelization. You should be in touch with a pastor who can complete the evangelization process by initiating the individual into full church life. The ultimate goal should always be to bring the evangelized into full communion with the body of Christ.

The fourth word, *dare,* is an obvious one. Many Christians fail to evangelize because they are afraid to. We can be afraid of rejection, of hostile words, of ridicule. These are normal human fears. We need to accept them and to conquer them by seeking the Lord's help. Like Peter stepping out of the boat, when we keep our eyes on Jesus fear diminishes and often vanishes altogether.

If we are to evangelize without fear, we need to request an anointing of the Holy Spirit. "The Spirit God has given us is no cowardly Spirit, but rather one that makes us strong, loving and wise" (2 Tm 1:17).

Our greatest fear is usually fear of rejection. The person we want to share the gospel with may not want to hear "religious" conversation. Our attempts to share what Jesus has done in our lives will be rejected or ridiculed. However, there are ways to minimize the risk of rejection. These ways are all associated with the word care that we have already discussed. When we demonstrate real care, real love for the person, the possibility of rejection diminishes greatly.

When all is said and done, we can trust the Holy Spirit to guide us as we respond to his prompting to share our faith with another person. Have a sincere, simple love for Jesus nourished by prayer. As you do, you will grow in your conviction that he is the most important person you could ever want someone to meet. The rest will come naturally.

Another key element in evangelization is making disciples of the men and women we evangelize. In the gospel passage I quoted earlier from St. Matthew, you will notice that Jesus says "make disciples of all the nations." He doesn't want us just to make converts, to lead others into belief. He wants them to be disciples and often he wants us to be involved in that process. Whenever possible, we are to bring the people we evangelize to the same sort of commitment of disciple-ship that we have. Evangelism is so important a part of the life of the disciple that I urge each reader to seek out someone to witness to immediately. In fact, I want to challenge every disciple reading this book to seek to make one new disciple during the next three months. By that I mean to bring someone you know who is not a believer or who is a lukewarm Christian into a vibrant relationship with Jesus Christ and to follow that victory by instilling in them the desire to grow as a disciple of the Lord.

Once you have that one success, go back to the Lord and ask him to give you another person to evangelize. Before long you will have made evangelism part of your life and you will have taken another giant step in your growth as a disciple.

Evangelism is so important because God's plan is that the world be changed by people being changed. A lot of people invest time and energy into trying to change social structures. The truth is that changed people change structures. We should invest our ener-gies in trying to change the people through a disciple-ship relationship with Jesus Christ.

Discipleship—yours and that of those new disciples you introduce to the Lord—is not a one-time affair. It is a whole new way of life. In the passage from Matthew Jesus continues to say of these new disciples: "baptize them in the name of the Father and of the Son and of the Holy Spirit."

The Lord wants all disciples to come into church

life. He wants them to be part of the sacramental life of the community of faith. He wants them to understand that their relationship with Father, Son, and Spirit is personal but that it is also nourished with ritual worship, with preaching, and with fellowship. These are available only in a church environment.

Then Jesus says, "Teach them." We need teaching as part of our personal formation as disciples. The people we are introducing to the disciple's way of life also need teaching. Coming to know Jesus Christ as your Lord and Savior, as wonderful as it is, is only the beginning—the moment of rebirth into this new way of life. From then on we need to be in a formation program that continues until we see him face to face.

Sometimes this will mean that we will be their teachers, sometimes not. We will need to be very sensitive to the Lord in this regard. We must be careful not to smother those we have nurtured in faith and keep our egos out of the way. New Christians may need someone besides us to teach them. In fact, just as children grow up and leave their parents after having learned how to function in the adult world, most of the people we have introduced to the Lord will leave us. We have to be ready for that to happen and willing to accept it.

This discussion concludes with the last verse of the Gospel of Matthew. It is one of the most encouraging and most edifying passages in the Bible: "Know that I am with you always until the end of the world."

Our entire faith, all our hope, our discipleship are based on that phrase. He is with us, always! The truth that we stand on is that once we have given our lives to Jesus Christ and had that covenant relationship sealed with his blood and by the power of the Holy Spirit, nothing can separate us from his love and his grace. He is with us! And therein lies our security. He will never abandon us, not even for a moment. He is always with us, until the end.

TEN

Salt and Light

WE NOW TURN OUR ATTENTION to the disciple's relationship to the world. The word of God has a great deal to say about this, and we will examine some of scripture's teaching. But first, let us take stock of what kind of world we Christian disciples find ourselves in during the last part of the twentieth century.

The problems facing our world today are caused by our fallen nature. We are sinners; the sons and daughters of sinners; and our flesh is weak and prone to sinfulness. The lures of the world and the wiles of the Devil are the other two potent enemies of the Christian disciple.

We face these enemies in our daily lives, but they also affect the way we relate to the larger body of Christ and to the non-Christian people and environments we all have to face.

How are we as disciples supposed to cope with all

the human difficulties that surround us? How can we confront social ills with the gospel?

Jesus told us how: "You are the salt of the earth" (Mt 5:13).

We have all heard that passage. But what exactly did Jesus mean? Salt serves two useful purposes: it flavors and it preserves certain kinds of food. Without salt, many of the foods we eat would not taste very good. Even more important, without salt many kinds of food would spoil before they were eaten. The preservative function of salt was more important in the past. Before the development of refrigeration and other forms of preserving food, salt was vital to human survival. Even today salt is very important to us as a preservative and a flavorer.

Jesus had both of these characteristics of salt in mind when he told his disciples that they were to be the salt of the earth. He was telling them that they were to preserve the spiritual life. They were to live according to spiritual values and to accomplish spiritual good in a world where both were in danger of falling to paganism, to strife, and to superficial religious practice.

Jesus was also telling his disciples that they would "spice things up" in the world as they followed his word and built his church. Even a brief look at the history of the apostolic age shows how true this is. The disciples caused consternation wherever they went. They were opposed by Jews, Romans, and just about everyone else they came in contact with. When disciples gathered riots often followed. But the teaching and the lifestyle of the disciples also attracted many people to the Christian faith. They were spicing things up because the Son of God himself was working through them.

Today God wants his disciples to be salt to our generation.

In the present historical moment, with all of its difficulties and all of its promise, God desires to raise up a group of people who are holding things together. By the way they live, by the style of our lives, by being disciples of the Lord Jesus Christ, we can truly be the salt that is so much needed to preserve many important things which are now in jeopardy.

In his letter on evangelization, Pope Paul VI made an observation that is pertinent to this discussion:

For the Church, evangelizing means bringing the Good News into all the strata of humanity, and through its influence transforming humanity from within and making it new: "Now I am making the whole of creation new" [Rv 21:5]. But there is no new humanity if there are not first of all new persons renewed by Baptism and by lives lived according to the Gospel. The purpose of evangelization is therefore precisely this interior change, and if it had to be expressed in one sentence the best way of stating it would be to say that the Church evangelizes when she seeks to convert, solely through the divine power of the message she proclaims, both the personal and collective consciences of people, the activities in which they engage, and the lives and concrete milieux which are theirs.

You and I as disciples have a very special mission to be men and women of influence. God wants us to exert influence not only in our churches but also in our society and in our government; in the marketplace and the schools; in our places of employment and recreation; in medicine and law and other important professions. Wherever we happen to be as disciples of the Lord, we are to have influence.

We are not supposed to be men and women who are letting history happen to us. We are supposed to be happening to history. God wants to equip us and lead us forth in mighty ways that will actually *make* history. We are not to wake up in the morning and allow life just to occur to us. We are to be aggressive, outgoing, and assertive in desiring to change things in accord with the principles we have learned in the word of God.

This is a big responsibility. But it is something that we can do naturally because of the grace and the gifts we have received through the Holy Spirit.

Now I know that some people feel powerless to make a difference even in their own families, let alone in organizations as imposing as the local school board, the American Medical Association, or the U.S. Congress. But powerlessness is not something we need to worry about. We are disciples of the great King of the universe. We have the same power at our disposal that fashioned heaven and earth. There is no power shortage in the kingdom of God!

Let me tell you a story of modern, ordinary people who are experiencing the power of God in absolutely profound ways.

No one in the world is more powerless than the poor people who live in the teeming cities in countries of the Third World. These people struggle every day just to get a few morsels of food. I am not exaggerating when I say this. Millions of people the world over struggle each day just for a few mouthfuls of food. Often even a few mouthfuls are denied them.

But I know of a group of poor people in Juarez, Mexico, who are not only being fed and clothed, but are coming to know the Lord Jesus Christ and are rising above the indignity of their poverty. All this has come about because a small group of disciples in El Paso, Texas, heard God's voice and obeyed.

One morning a group of women sitting in their comfortable American home in El Paso studying the scripture were prompted by the Holy Spirit to look across the Rio Grande river and see the suffering of the Mexican people in Juarez. The women knew of the poverty in Juarez; everyone in El Paso does. But the Lord gave them new eyes to see with. They knew that if the Lord wanted them to serve the needy people across the border, he would give them the resources to do it with.

This happened a few days before Thanksgiving Day. At first the women thought the Lord wanted them to do up holiday baskets for the poor as many generous people across the United States do at Thanksgiving and Christmas. But the Lord had much more than this in mind. A short time later the women came in contact with a Jesuit priest, Father Rick Thomas, who developed a vision of forming a community of Christian people in El Paso whose major work would be to feed hungry people in Juarez.

The community, headquartered at Our Lady's Youth Center in El Paso, has been going strong for more than ten years now. It operates the Lord's Food Bank at two locations in Juarez. Approximately 2,000 Mexican families receive their basic food supplies from the food banks, but only after working several hours to pay for it.

The community also conducts a medical and dental clinic, ministers inside prisons and mental hospitals, and fills other needs of the poor as they arise.

People who would be starving now have enough food to eat.

However, the disciples who work with Father Thomas never forget that as important as feeding hungry people is, the first priority is to evangelize the people. All of the Juarez activities are geared around evangelism and prayer. Thousands of people have come to know and love and serve the Lord Jesus Christ as a result of this ministry.

There is power when a group of disciples discover the fullness of life and ministry in the Lord Jesus Christ. There is power in the enlightenment that comes from the study of God's word. There is power in good pastoral leadership. With these building blocks of God's power in place in our lives, any group of disciples, no matter how poor they are or how little education or social status they may have, they can change even great problems because of God's power. Events in El Paso and Juarez have proven that to me.

We are not just salt. Jesus tells his disciples that "You are the light of the world" (Mt 5:14).

The Lord knows that there is a lot of darkness in the world. The Lord knows that there is a lot of oppression. The Lord knows that there are many kinds of personal and social difficulty. He knows it because he was one of us. He knows it because it is the fruit of sin and of the warfare of the evil one—the Lord's eternal enemy—against human beings.

But the Lord gives us a remedy for darkness: we can be light itself. We can have the light of Christ shining so brightly in our lives that darkness cannot overcome it. Jesus Christ is calling men and women, young and old, all nationalities, all types and sizes, to be the light of the world.

Jesus inflames his disciples with the desire to love and serve. He sets us on fire with this desire, and then he sends his Holy Spirit to be for us the power to serve. The Holy Spirit is the fuel which keeps the fire of

Christ burning in our hearts. The Holy Spirit is the wisdom and the strength which keeps us moving forward effectively.

Christian disciples are to be filled with enthusiasm. I am not talking about some kind of contrived emotionalism which comes and goes like the fickle wind. Disciples are not people who just go around like cheerleaders, trying to whip us emotional enthusiasm. We are people who are called to live in a special kind of relationship with Jesus Christ so that he leads us and guides us into the positions of influence that he wants us to have. Because he is leading us, we can be authentically enthusiastic, throwing ourselves into the work with everything we have because it is the work of the Master whom we love more than life itself.

But rememeber: It is only by living in a daily relationship of prayer, discernment, and obedience that we can effectively throw God's eternal light on the situations Christ leads us into.

So far I've only talked theoretically about being salt and light. All this theory has very practical implications for the lives of disciples. The principles of salt and light apply first of all to our behavior towards those we live with every day. Are we salt and light to spouse and children, to parents, to coworkers?

The workplace is a great place of challenge for Christian disciples. Do we use every opportunity to witness about Jesus Christ to coworkers? Do we follow all of his teachings as we deal with all the situations we confront at our place of employment?

These questions apply to everyone who holds a job. But I think they apply even more urgently to men and women who hold positions of responsibility. Examine your life, disciples of the Lord, and see if you are being salt and light at home, in your church, and in your place of work.

The next important area is involvement in the world beyond our home and workplace.

Some of you disciples may be called into the very major step of entering the political arena by running for public office or entering government. It is a great calling to use one's Christianity to influence the political processes of our nation.

I know of a group of ordinary Christian men who work at ordinary jobs who became active in the county organization of one of the major political parties. Their sole purpose was to begin to exert Christian influence on this political party which, in their county, was secular and worldly. It has been difficult for these men; the people they work with don't change quickly. But they have hung in there for several years and they are beginning to see the fruit of their labor in local politics. Eventually, that fruit might be felt on the state and even the federal level.

While God is probably only calling a few of us to political activity, there are many other types of service that are appropriate for Christians. Some may be called to become involved in the PTA at school or to become influential with the local school board. Christian voices must be heard in the planning of curriculum for our schools.

Some will be called to volunteer time to important social service groups such as those that serve in the right-to-life cause. There are many prolife agencies and alternatives-to-abortion groups that need volunteers to help in the fight against the horrendous evil of abortion that afflicts our society.

There are many other great causes that disciples of Jesus Christ are called to work in. Some of these are prison ministries like Chuck Colson's Prison Fellowship, groups such as the St. Vincent de Paul Society which serve the materially needy, and the various ministries which spread the good news of Jesus Christ through evangelization.

No matter how simple or how lofty the calling Jesus places on our lives, it involves choice on our part. We choose to hear his call, to respond to it day after day, and to remain faithful to his principles regardless of the temptations that arise in our field of service. We have to choose each morning when we wake up to turn to the Lord and give him our entire day—everything we will do, think, and say. We ask him again to be Lord of our lives, to assert his proper role as our Lord and Savior.

We must also choose each and every day to be positive, to be loving, to smile, to care, to offer a friendly "hello" to everyone we meet. We must also choose to be aware of the needs of those around us. Give a drink of water to a thirsty person and a helping hand to a needy person. Embrace the person hungering for affection. Visit a person hospitalized or shut-in or imprisoned.

Being salt and light to the world isn't always dramatic, but it often is. If more of us did it we would see whole neighborhoods change. I have seen it happen more than once. We would see changes in social order and great growth in evangelism.

The Christian churches are so lacking in influence today because we have not discovered the light, the salt, the flavor, the energy, the enthusiasm, and the power that comes when dozens and scores and hundreds of ordinary Christians are motivated to react in positive, godly ways to people and events and situations they confront in daily life.

We know that this power, this enthusiasm, this energy can only come through the Holy Spirit. The flame of Pentecost should burn in our hearts each day. Jesus Christ desires his disciples to be filled with the Holy Spirit, to be immersed in the Holy Spirit, to be baptized in the Holy Spirit. The light, the salt, and the influence comes from what happens inside us as we are filled with the Holy Spirit and manifest his gifts.

Listen to these the words of our Master, as a discipline of discipleship: "Your light must shine before men, so that they may see goodness in your acts and give praise to your heavenly Father" (Mt 5:16).

My friends, we are to be visible. Our light is not to be hidden under a basket. We have an awesome responsibility to do good things in such a way that the men and women we encounter will be moved by them and will give praise to our heavenly Father. Our goodness will bear fruit, not only in our hearts, not only in social changes, but in others. It will lead many around us to acknowledge God as Father and to turn their lives over to him as we have.

We are to do all this with servants' hearts, especially to build up the lives of other people.

Consider the following passage:

> Jesus then called them together and said, "You know how those who exercise authority among the Gentiles lord it over them. Their great ones make their importance felt. It cannot be like that with you. Anyone among you who aspires to greatness must serve the rest. And whoever wants to rank first among you must serve the needs of all. Such is the case with the Son of Man, who has not come to be served by others, but to serve, to give his own life as a ransom for the many." (Mt 20:25-28)

Remember what Jesus our master did at the Last Supper. He girded himself and washed the feet of his disciples and then he said: "Do you understand what I just did for you? You address me as "Teacher" and "Lord" and fittingly enough, for that is what I am. But if I washed your feet, I who am Teacher and Lord— then you must wash each others' feet" (Jn 13:12-14).

When we let the Lord disciple us, and help us to develop an attitude of serving, life really becomes more exciting. It also becomes more tolerable, because one of the great problems among us because of our human pride is that we want to be on top of everything. We want to lord it over and we want to have all the answers.

But Jesus Christ says, you will find happiness when you serve in my name and for my sake. The Lord came that we might have life and have it more abundantly. And part of that abundant living is the fulfillment, meaning, joy, direction, and happiness, that comes from being his disciples and being formed into servants of his people.

ELEVEN

Radicals for Christ

W E ARE PRIVILEGED to be part of one of the most spiritually dynamic periods in the history of the church. The last half of the twentieth century has seen spiritual activity which goes beyond any era I am aware of. This spiritual dynamism is a work of the Holy Spirit.

Why has God chosen our generation to be a time of spiritual revival? No human can answer that question. We simply don't know exactly what God has in mind. But we can guess. Some guess that the end of the world is at hand. I don't know about that myself. The best guess I can offer is that God has chosen our era, with all its great strengths and all its horrifying weaknesses, to be a pivotal time in salvation history. There have been pivotal times before. One of these occurred in the fourth century when the Roman imperor Constantine halted the persecution of Christians and made Christianity the state religion. Another pivotal time was the great spiritual revival in Europe spearheaded by St. Francis of Assisi and St. Dominic during the twelfth century. Another was the Reformation, when the fabric of Christian unity was tragically shredded but was followed by spiritual vitality in the new Protestant churches and in the Roman Catholic Church as well.

God has been active in the lives of men and women during each of these eras. The Holy Spirit has produced great good, moving the church on towards its destiny of becoming the spotless and holy bride of Jesus Christ.

The spiritual renewal occurring during our own age seems to be as important as any or them; perhaps more so.

Yet throughout the world, many men and women have yet to make the choice to accept Jesus Christ into their lives. God is offering a special time of grace today. He is offering human beings eternal life and abundant life on earth. But to receive it, each person has to make a choice to believe in Christ, to renounce sin, to turn away from the world, and to follow Christian teaching. That's not new, of course. It is the centuries-old teaching of Christianity. But today, God has raised up more evangelistic vehicles than ever before to proclaim this message throughout the world. Many more men and women around the globe are being confronted with the gospel than ever before. This time of revival is bearing great fruit in many places, especially in the poorer countries in Africa, Asia, and Latin America where the church is growing at unprecedented rates.

What is God calling you to? I cannot answer that for you. Only you can answer, with prayer, study, and proper pastoral care from the leaders of your local church community. I can't tell you what service the Lord has in mind for you, but I can tell you something about the attitude you must have to serve Jesus Christ as his disciple. You must be selflessly dedicated to the cause of the kingdom of God.

Several years ago a letter a young man had written to his fiance came to my attention. This young man was a dedicated disciple, not of Jesus Christ, but of Communism. He was breaking off his engagement because he felt that marriage would hinder his ability to work and sacrifice for the Communist Party.

Now, I don't believe that Communism is a good thing. In fact, I believe quite the opposite. I am sharing this letter not to make Communism look good, but to give an example of the kind of dedication that we are called to as disciples of Jesus Christ:

> We Communists have a high casualty rate. We are the ones who get shot and hung and lynched and tarred and feathered and jailed and slandered and ridiculed, fired from our jobs, and in every other way made as uncomfortable as possible. A certain percentage of us get killed or imprisoned. We live in virtual poverty. We turn back to the Party every penny we make above what is absolutely necessary to keep us alive. We Communists don't have the time or the money for many movies or concerts or T-bone

steaks or decent homes or new cars. We have been described as fanatics. We are fanatics. Our lives are dominated by one overshadowing factor—the struggle for world Communism. We Communists have a philosophy of life which no amount of money could buy. We have a cause to fight for, a definite purpose in life. We subordinate our petty personal selves to a great movement of humanity and if our personal lives seem hard or our egos seem to suffer through subordination to the Party, then we are adequately compensated by the thought that each of us, in his small way, is contributing something new and true and better for mankind. There is one thing about which I am in dead earnest and that is the Communist cause.

That's a powerful statement of this man's dedication. Unfortunately it is to an evil cause. It should indicate to us, disciples of Jesus Christ, the kind of dedication we are to have to the cause of the kingdom of our Master.

We need to be fanatics too—fanatics for the cause of Jesus Christ. We must be ready, willing, and able at any moment to offer whatever God asks of us—our time, our money—setting aside our personal desires and comfort. But we need to be careful about how we express our fanaticism. God does not want us to cause grave upset to our families, or to cause scandal to his name by doing things that don't make good sense.

For example, a woman once came to me and said,

"God is calling me to leave my husband so that I can devote full-time to my ministry of evangelism and healing. I don't have anything against him, it's just that God is calling me on." That woman certainly was not hearing God correctly. She was preparing to leave her husband, her home, her family, and her children for her perceived "ministry." That's nonsense.

I don't know if the woman had a ministry or not. Maybe she did. If so, God probably wanted her to exercise it first of all within her family. If she cared so little for her husband and children, they could well have been in need of healing. I doubt that God wanted the woman out on the road conducting healing services in the name of the Lord of love while she exhibited so little love in her own life.

That's not the kind of commitment that God calls for. He calls for a much more difficult kind—daily commitment to prayer and service within the context of the family or church community in which he has placed us.

The kind of commitment I am talking about is the kind I saw in action one year at a national Catholic charismatic renewal conference at the University of Notre Dame. The conference theme concerned the Christian family, and parents were encouraged to bring their children. Many did, including a man who had a son who was severely mentally handicapped.

People who go to conferences stand in a lot of long lines. They stand in line to register, to get their meals, and so forth. They also sit for long periods of time—

three hours or more. If you have a mentally handicapped child on your lap, you can't get up and move around too freely.

This man had probably held that boy while standing in lines. He had certainly held him on his lap for hours on the Saturday I saw him. Yet when I saw that man and the look of love on his face as he wiped his son's mouth, I saw the kind of commitment that God wants us to have for the eternal kingdom. When we are committed enough to sacrifice our own comfort, our own needs for those of someone else, we are the kind of person that Jesus Christ can use to build his kingdom.

I have used some heavy words here. I've said we need to be radicals and fanatics. I have one more heavy word that disciples of Jesus Christ should be familiar with: revolution. Christianity is the revolution that ought to be taking place in the world. We know the great needs of men and women today. We also know the truth. The only way to get the truth to the people with the needs is through spiritual revolution that is manifested in Christian action.

Even now God is searching his people. Where will he find the kind of dedication needed for revolution? Among the disciples? This is our call. We as children of the light should lay down our lives for Jesus Christ and his gospel of love and peace.

Other Books and Tapes
by Fr. John Bertolucci

On Fire With the Spirit
My personal story
$4.95

Share the Good News
$.95

Spreading the Good News
(four cassette album)
$24.95

Preaching the Gospel
(four cassette album)
$24.95

The Fr. John Bertolucci Testimony
(single cassette)
$5.95

Charismatic Life in the Catholic Liturgy
(single cassette)
$5.95

Praise, Healing, and Renewal in the Eucharist
(single cassette)
$5.95

Available at your Christian bookstore or from:

**Servant Publications • Dept. 209 • P.O. Box 7455
Ann Arbor, Michigan 48107**

Please include payment plus $.75 per book
for postage and handling

*Send for your FREE catalog of Christian
books, music, and cassettes.*